INJU[illegible] AND THE UNJUST

SHAYKH MUHAMMAD MITWALLI
AL-SHA'RAWI

DAR AL-TAQWA

ISBN 1-870582-37-3

Translation: Aisha Bewley

Editors: Abdalhaqq Bewley and Muhammad Isa Waley

Production: Bookwork, Norwich

Published by:
Dar Al Taqwa Ltd.
7A Melcombe Street
Baker Street
London NW1 6AE

Printed in England by De-Luxe Printers Ltd.
245a, Acton Lane, London NW10 7NR
email: deluxeprinters1@aol.com
Tel.: 020 8965 1771

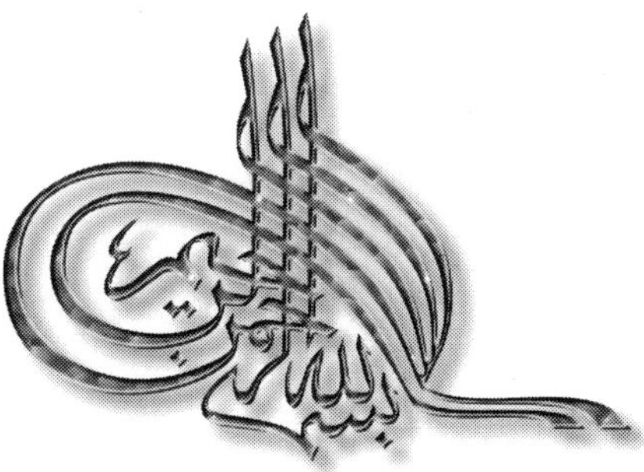

In the name of God, most Gracious, most Merciful

Table of Contents

Injustice and the Unjust

Muhammad Mitwalli ash-Sha‘rawi

In the name of Allah, the All-Merciful, Most Merciful

Publisher's Foreword

Praise be to Allah. We praise Him, seek His help and ask His forgiveness. We seek refuge with Allah from the evil of ourselves and from our evil deeds. "*If Allah misguides someone, he has no guide and if Allah guides someone, he cannot be misguided.*" (39:37) I testify that there is no god but Allah alone with no partner and I testify that Muhammad is His slave and Messenger.

"*You who believe! Be fearful of Allah with the fear that is His due and do not die except as Muslims.*" (3:104)

"*O Mankind! Be fearful of your Lord who created you from a single self and created its mate from it and then disseminated many men and women from the two of them. Be fearful of Allah in whose name you make demands on one another and also be fearful of Him in respect of your families. Allah watches over you continually.*" (4:1)

"*O you who believe! Be fearful of Allah and speak words which hit the mark. He will put your actions right for you and forgive you your wrong deeds. All who obey Allah and His Messenger have won a mighty victory.*" (33:70-71)

The truest of words are the words of Allah and the best guidance is the guidance of Muhammad, may Allah bless him and grant him peace. The worst of matters are new ones. Every new matter is an innovation and every innovation is misguidance and every misguidance is in the Fire.

1. The creature most loved by Allah

It is related that Ibn Mas'ud, may Allah be pleased with him, said, "The Messenger of Allah, may Allah bless him and grant him peace, said, 'All creatures are dependants of Allah and the most beloved of creatures to Allah is the one who is best to his dependants.'"

Al-'Ajluni said in *Kashf al-khafa'* (1220): "At-Tabarani related it in *al-Kabir* and *al-Awsat*, Abu Nu'aym in *Hilya al-Awliya'*, and al-Bayhaqi in *ash-Shi'ab* as *marfu'* from Ibn Mas'ud ﷺ".

Abu Nu'aym related it, as did Abu Ya'la, at-Tabarani, al-Bazzar, Ibn Abi Dunya, and others related it as *marfu'* from Anas ﷺ.

At-Tabarani related it from Ibn Mas'ud ﷺ as: "The most beloved of creatures to Allah is the one who is of most benefit to his dependants."

Ad-Daylami related it from Anas as *a marfu'* report with the words: "All creatures are dependants of Allah and under His protection, and the most beloved of creatures to Allah is the one who is best to his dependants."

In the transmission of al-'Askari from Ibn 'Umar ﷺ is that he said, "It was asked, 'Messenger of Allah, which person is most beloved to Allah?' He answered, 'The most beneficial of people to other people.'"

At-Tabarani has a *marfu'* report from Zayd ibn Khalid: "The best action is that which is beneficial, the best guidance is that which is followed, and the best of people is the one most beneficial to other people."

It is attributed to Anas in *ad-Durar* by al-Bayhaqi in *ash-Shi'ab* and Abu Ya'la with a weak *isnad.*

Ibn 'Adi reported from Ibn Mas'ud ﷺ with the words: "All creatures are dependants of Allah, and the most beloved of them to Him is the most beneficial to his dependants."

An-Nawawi said in his *Fatwas* that it is a weak *hadith* because its *isnad* contains Yusuf ibn 'Atiyya, who the Imams agree is weak.

Al-Hafiz 'Abdu'l-'Adhim al-Mundhiri related it *marfu'* in his *Forty Hadiths* from Anas as: "All creatures are dependants of Allah, and the most beloved of His creation to Him is the one who is the most beneficial to his dependants."

Abu 'Abdullah as-Sulami reported in his exegesis: "The dependants of Allah are the poor in need of Allah. All creatures are in need of Allah. He is the One who tends to them."

The *hadith* has different paths of transmission which reinforce one another.

Al-'Askari said, "These words are metaphorical and can be expanded on. It is as if since Allah is responsible for providing for His slaves and in charge of them so all creatures are like His dependants. Similar to that is the *hadith* which begins: "Allah has two families among mankind: the people of the Qur'an, who are the people of Allah..."[1]

How excellent are these words of Abu'l-'Atahiyya:

Among the dependants of Allah the noblest in His sight
    is the one who is more generous to his dependants.
We have not seen any praise for someone who acts
    more eloquent than his own actions.

Another said:

All creation are the dependants of Allah
    and under His protection.
The one he loves the most
    is the one kindest to his dependants.

At-Tayyibi, writing in *as-Saghir,* said:

The best of the slaves of Allah
    is the one most beneficial to them.
Every *faqih* has related this from the Companions.
The God of the Throne, may He be exalted,
    helps the youth as long as he helps his brother.

According to Ibn Hajar al-Makki in *Fatawa al-Hadithiyya*: "The *hadith* which says: 'Created beings are the dependants of Allah, and the most beloved of them to Him is the one who is the most beneficial to his dependants,' is related by paths, all of which are weak. One of them has, 'All creatures are the dependants of Allah and under His protection, so the most beloved of creatures to Allah is the one who is best to his dependants, and

1. Ibn Majah (215). Al-Albani says that it is sound.

the most hated of creatures to Allah is the one who is most inhibiting to his dependants.'"

2. Allah honours the sons of Adam

Allah Almighty says, *"We have honoured the sons of Adam and conveyed them on land and sea and provided them with good things, and have favoured them greatly over many We have created."* (17:70)

Al-Qurtubi said, "The words of Allah *'We have honoured'* are from the intensive form *karrama*, and mean: 'We have given them honour and excellence.' This is the honour which is the negation of imperfection, not the honour of wealth. This honour includes His creating them in this structure with an upright stature and a beautiful form and His conveying them on land and sea. It is not appropriate for any animal except the children of Adam to be carried by His will, intention and management. He singled them out for special foods, drinks and clothes. No other animal enjoys the same scope in this respect which the sons of Adam enjoy because they earn wealth which animals do not, and wear clothes and eat complex foods. The goal of every animal is to eat fresh meat or fodder which is not complex."

According to at-Tabari: "Allah says, *'We have honoured the sons of Adam'* by giving them authority over other creatures and subjecting all creation to them. *'We conveyed them on land'* on the backs of animals and conveyances *'and on the sea'* in boats which We subject to them. *'We provided them with good things'* in terms of food and drink. They are what is lawful and tasty. *"We favoured them greatly over many We have created'* by giving them the ability to work with their hands, and carry their food and drink with them, and lift it to their mouths. That is not easy for other creatures except them."

We read in the *Summary of the Commentary of Ibn Kathir* by as-Sabuni: "Allah reports how He honoured and esteemed the sons of Adam by His creating them on the best and most perfect form, as He says, *'We created man in the finest form'* (95:4), meaning that he walks upright on his feet and eats with his hands while other animals walk on all fours and eat with their mouths. He gave him hearing, sight and a heart; by means of those things he has understanding and uses it and distinguishes between things and realises their beneficial and harmful properties with regard to matters of both the *deen* and this world.

" *'We conveyed them on land'* means on animals like oxen, horses, and mules; *'and sea'* refers to ships of all sizes. *'We have provided them with good things'* meaning crops, fruits, meat and milk, and all sorts of foods with their delicious varieties. The *'good things'* also include good appearance and fine clothes of all sorts with their different categories, colours and shapes which people make for themselves and which other people bring them from different regions and areas. *'We have favoured them greatly over many We have created'* means over other animals and categories of creatures.

"This noble *ayat* is used as evidence of the superiority of human beings over the angels. It is reported from 'Abdullah ibn 'Amr that the Prophet ﷺ stated, 'The angels said, "O our Lord! You gave the sons of Adam this world in which they eat and drink and dress. We glorify your praise and do not eat or drink or play. As you gave them this world, give us the Next World!" He said, 'I will not make the righteous descendants of those I created with My own hands like the one to whom I said "Be" and he was."'[1] Al-Hafiz at-Tabarani related this and 'Abdu'r-Razzaq transmitted it from Zayd ibn Muslim as *mawquf* and Ibn 'Asakir from Anas ibn Malik as *marfu'*.

3. Allah's Blessing upon Man

Following the directions which Allah has written for him, the believer is able to see the effects of Allah's mercy and blessing in everything around him. As for the blessings of Allah on him in

1. Al-Haythami said in *Majma' az-Zawa'id* (265) that at-Tabarani related this in *al-Kabir* and *al-Awsat*. Its *isnad* contains Ibrahim ibn 'Abdullah ibn Khalid al-Mahisi who is a liar whose words are to be disregarded. The *isnad* in *al-Awsat* contains Talha ibn Zayd who is also a liar.

his person, they are even greater and more extraordinary. The first of them is the blessing of creation itself. If it had not been for Allah's will and favour, we would have remained in the darkness of non-existence and would not have been anything remembered: *"Has man ever known a point of time when he was not something remembered? We created man from a mingled drop to test him, and We made him hearing and seeing."* (76:1-3)

The second is the blessing of humanity. Allah wished to create a well-formed human being and to establish him in the earth; and He preferred him over all His creatures. *"We have honoured the sons of Adam and conveyed them on land and sea, and provided them with good things and favoured them greatly over many We have created."* (17:70) Allah followed that with excellence of spiritual and physical form: *"We created man in the finest form"* (85:4) and *"He formed you, giving you the best of forms."* (64:3).

The third is the blessing of perception and knowledge. Allah Almighty says: *"Recite: And your Lord is the Most Generous, He who taught by the pen, taught man what he did not know."* (96:3-5) The Almighty says, *"Allah brought you out of your mothers' wombs knowing nothing at all, and gave you hearing, sight and hearts so that perhaps you might show thanks."* (16:78) These three faculties are the means by which we gain knowledge and are our organs of perception.

The fourth is the blessing of speech and writing. The Almighty says, *"The All-Merciful taught the Qur'an. He created man and taught him clear expression."* (55:1-4) The Almighty says, *"He who taught by the pen"* (95:4) and the Almighty says, "Nun. *By the Pen and what they write down!"* (68:1)

The fifth is the blessing of provision. The Almighty says, *"O mankind! Remember Allah's blessing upon you. Is there any Creator other than Allah providing for you from heaven and earth?"* (35:3); the Almighty also says, *"Say: 'Who provides for you from the heavens and earth?' Say: 'Allah.'"* (34:24)

The sixth is particular to believers. It is the blessing of faith and guidance to the Straight Path of Allah. *"Know that the Messenger of Allah is among you. If he were to obey you in many things, you would suffer for it. But Allah has given you love of faith and made it pleasing to your hearts, and has made unbelief, degeneracy and disobedience hateful to you. People such as these are rightly-guided. It is a great favour from Allah and a blessing. Allah is All-Knowing, All-Wise."* (49:7-8) The Almighty says, "*They think they have done you a favour by becoming Muslims! Say: 'Do not consider your Islam a favour to me. No indeed! It is Allah who has favoured you by guiding you to belief if you are truthful.'"* (49:17)

The seventh is the blessing of brotherhood and love. *"Remember Allah's blessing upon you when you were enemies and He joined your hearts together so that you became brothers by His blessing."* (3:103) Allah says, *"He brought their hearts together. Even if you had spent everything in the earth, you could not have brought their hearts together. But Allah has brought them together. He is Almighty, All-Wise."* (8:63)

4. A Muslim should not wrong another Muslim or hand him over

Al-Bukhari (2310) related from 'Abdullah ibn 'Umar ﵁ that the Messenger of Allah ﷺ said, "The Muslim is the brother of the Muslim. He should not wrong him or hand him over to his enemy. Allah will take care of the needs of anyone who takes care of the needs of his brother. On the Day of Rising Allah will dispel the anxiety of anyone who dispels the anxiety of another Muslim. On the Day of Rising Allah will veil anyone who veils another Muslim."[1]

Al-Hafiz Ibn Hajar said in *Fath al-Bari*, "His words, 'The Muslim is the brother of another Muslim' refers to the brotherhood of Islam. Every harmony between two things is called 'brotherhood'. That is shared by free and slave, one adult and those with discernment.

"The words, 'He should not wrong him' is in the form of a statement which implies a command. It is *haram* for one Muslim to wrong another. The words 'or hand him over' means that he must not abandon him to anyone who will harm him or leave

1. Muslim, 58/2080.

him in a situation which will harm him. Rather he must help him and defend him. This is more particular than simply abandoning injustice. That can be mandatory or merely recommended, according to the difference in circumstances." At-Tabarani added by another line of narration from Salim, "He should not leave him in a calamity which has befallen him."

"The words 'Whoever veils a Muslim' refer to not disclosing him if one sees him doing something ugly. This does not entail not criticising what he is doing on a one-to-one basis. The command allows giving testimony against someone if honest criticism and advice do not stop him doing his ugly actions and he makes them public. Similarly, people are commanded to conceal bad things if they do them themselves, although it is not forbidden to go to the ruler and confess. It is clear that what should be concealed is disobedience which has come to an end. Objection, however, should be expressed in case someone continues to be engaged in disobedience. If that has no effect, the case should be taken to the relevant authorities. Doing so is not the kind of slander which is forbidden, it is rather part of mandatory good counsel. The *hadith* also indicates that people should not slander others, because whoever makes public the evils of his brother, thus committing slander, has certainly not veiled him.

"His words, 'On the Day of Rising Allah will veil anyone' are reported in the *hadith* of Abu Hurayra related by at-Tirmidhi as 'Allah will veil him in this world and the Next"'.

The *hadith* contains encouragement to people to help one another and be good companions and friends. It also indicates that the reward received is in accordance with the act of obedience practised and that whoever swears that so-and-so is his brother, meaning the brotherhood of Islam, has not broken his oath.

Al-Mubarakpuri said in *Tuhfatu'l-Awadhi,* "In the *hadith* related from Ibn 'Umar the words 'Whoever veils a Muslim' can refer to his actual person or else to his fault – by not slandering him and hiding his faults. This is in respect of someone not known for corruption. Otherwise, it is recommended to convey information about him to the ruler. When someone sees acts of disobedience, he should object to them in any way possible. If he cannot do that he should present it to the authorities.

5. Making things easy for a Muslim

It is related that Abu Hurayra ﷺ said that the Messenger of Allah ﷺ said, "If anyone relieves his brother of one of the afflictions of this world, Allah will relieve him of one of the afflictions of the Day of Rising. Allah will give ease in this world and the Next to anyone who eases the hardship of another. Allah will veil anyone who veils another Muslim in this world and the Next. Allah will help His slave as long as His slave is helping his brother. If anyone travels a path by which he seeks knowledge, Allah will make the way to the Garden easy for him. People do not meet in the mosque to recite the Book of Allah and study it together without tranquillity descending on them, mercy covering them, and the angels encircling them. If someone is slow in acting by it, his ascription to it is not hastened."[1]

Al-Mubarakpuri said in *Tuhfat'l-Awadhi*, "'If anyone relieves his brother of one of the afflictions of this world,' means 'removes it from him and relieves him of it'."

At-Tayyibi said, "It is as if he had opened someone's trachea enabling them to breathe. It is similar to the saying, 'You are in breath.' It is as if their calamity was like something blocking the trachea. When they are relieved of it they can breathe again. What is meant by 'brother' is brother in faith."

According to a variant reading of the *hadith* found in Muslim, "If anyone relieves a believer of one of the afflictions of the Day of Rising, Allah will relieve him." Since all creatures are the dependants of Allah and relieving affliction is doing good, Allah repays the person who does that with an ample repayment; as Allah says, *"Shall the recompense for doing good be other than consummate good?"* (55:60)

1. Muslim 36/2699 and at-Tirmidhi 2945.

The words "Anyone who veils a Muslim" refers to veiling the ugly actions which he does. One should not disgrace him or clothe him in a garment which Allah has concealed – in other words, reveal his faults or nakedness.

An-Nawawi said in his commentary on the words of the Prophet ﷺ, "On the Day of Rising, Allah will veil anyone who veils another Muslim":

> The veiling being recommended here is covering the faults and flaws of those who are not known for causing harm and corruption. In the case of one of those who are known for that, it is recommended not to veil them but that one present their case to those in authority, provided that one does not fear harm from doing it. That is because covering up for this sort of person encourages him to continue his harm, corruption, violation of sacred things, and inciting others to do similar actions. In any case the veiling referred to applies to acts of disobedience which occurred in the past and have now ended.
>
> If someone sees another actually involved in doing an act of disobedience, then he must hasten to object to it and forbid it to the best of his ability. It is not lawful to put off doing that. If he is unable to do it, he should report it to the authorities, provided that will not result in further corruption.
>
> The words "anyone who eases the hardship of another" refer to making things easy for someone who is poor, including both believers and unbelievers. In other words, if anyone is owed something by someone poor and one makes it easy for him by deferring it or forgoing some or all of it, "Allah will give him ease" in exchange for his making things easy for His slave, thus giving one repayment in kind.

In *Fayd al-Qadir*, the commentary on *al-Jami' as-Saghir*,[1] al-Munawi said:

1. A compilation of *hadiths* made by Jalal ad-din as-Suyuti.

The words "Anyone who veils another Muslim in this world" refer to veiling his ugly actions, and the words "does not disgrace him" mean by making known something which might cause him shame in respect of his *deen*, honour, property, or family. So you should not disgrace or expose him by talking about such things. The words "Allah will veil him on the Day of Rising" mean that He will not disgrace him in front of people by displaying his faults and wrong actions. On the contrary, Allah will make his reckoning easy and not punish him, since because He is Living and Generous. Veiling faults is one facet of modesty and generosity.

'Uthman summoned some suspect people and then sent a party out to arrest them, but they split up and he did not manage to capture them. He freed a slave out of thankfulness to Allah Almighty that the abasement of no Muslim should occur at his hands.

6. Injustice is darkness

It is related from 'Abdullah ibn 'Umar رضي الله عنه that the Prophet ﷺ said, "Injustice will be darkness on the Day of Rising." (al-Bukhari, 2315).

It is related from Jabir ibn 'Abdullah رضي الله عنه that the Prophet ﷺ said, "Beware of injustice. Injustice will be darkness on the Day of Rising. Beware of avarice. Avarice destroyed those before you and prompted them to shed each other's blood and make lawful what was unlawful." (Muslim 56/2578)

It is related from Abu Dharr رضي الله عنه that the Prophet ﷺ said in what he related from Allah Almighty, "O My slaves! I have forbidden injustice to Myself and I have made it unlawful between you, so do not wrong one another. O My slaves! All of you are misguided except those whom I guide, so seek My guidance and I will guide you. O My slaves! All of you are hungry except those that I feed, so ask me for food and I will feed you. O My slaves! All of you are naked except those that I clothe, so ask me for clothing and I will clothe you. O My slaves! You make mistakes by night and by day and I forgive all wrong action,s so ask for My forgiveness and I will forgive you. O My slaves! You will never attain to My harm so as to be able to harm Me and you will never attain to My benefit so as to be able to benefit Me. O My slaves! If the first and last of you, all the *jinn* and all the humans among you, possessed the heart of the most godfearing man among you, that would not increase My kingdom in any way. O My slaves! If the first and last of you, all the jinn and all the humans among you, possessed the heart of the most evil man among you, that would not diminish My kingdom in any way. O My slaves! If the first and last of you, all the *jinn* and all the humans among you, were to stand in a single place and ask of Me, I could give to every man what he asks without that decreasing what I have any more than a needle does when it enters the sea. O My slaves! It is your actions for which I call you to account and then repay you in full. So anyone who finds good should praise Allah; and anyone who finds something else should blame no one but himself." (Muslim, 55/2577)

Sa'id said, "When Abu Idris al-Khawlani related this *hadith*, he used to kneel."

Another variant reads, "I have forbidden injustice to Myself and My slaves, so do not wrong one another."

Anas reported that the Prophet ﷺ said, "Help your brother, wronging or wronged." We said, "Messenger of Allah, I can help someone wronged, but how can I help him if he is wronging?" He answered, "You restrain him from wronging. That is helping him."[1]

Qays stated, "Abu Bakr said after praising Allah and lauding him, 'O people! You recite this *ayat* and misinterpret it: *You are only responsible for yourselves. The misguided cannot harm you as long as you are guided.* (5:105) We heard the Prophet ﷺ declare, "When people see a wrongdoer and do not take hold of his hands, Allah is about to encompass them with a punishment." I heard the Messenger of Allah ﷺ say, "There are no people

1. At-Tirmidhi (2255); al-Albani described it as sound.

among whom acts of disobedience are done, and which they are able to change but fail to, but that Allah is about to encompass them with a punishment.'"

It is related that 'Abdullah ibn 'Amr ﷺ said, "I heard the Messenger of Allah ﷺ say, 'When you see my community too much in awe of wrongdoer to say to him, 'You are a wrongdoer' then bid farewell to them."[1]

It is related that al-Bara' ibn 'Azib ﷺ said, "A bedouin came to the Prophet ﷺ and said, 'Teach me an action which will admit me to the Garden.' He answered, 'Although the words are short, the question is broad. Free a soul and set free a slave.' He said, 'Messenger of Allah, are they not the same?' 'No,' he answered, 'Freeing a soul is that you alone set him free, and freeing a slave means that you help in freeing him by granting the use of the milk of an animal with milk and being kind to a relative who wrongs (you). If you cannot do that, then feed the hungry and give something to drink to the thirsty. Command the right and forbid the wrong. If you cannot do that, then withhold your tongue from anything but good."[2]

Thabit or Abu Thabit ﷺ related that a man entered the Damascus Mosque and said, "O Allah, turn my alienation into familiarity, show mercy to me in my exile, and provide me with a righteous companion." Abu'd-Darda' heard him and said, "If you are speaking the truth, then we are happier at what you have said than you are. I heard the Messenger of Allah ﷺ say, *'But some of them wrong themselves;'* (35:32) this refers to wrongdoers who will be punished in their situation by suffering much care and sorrow; *'and some are ambivalent;'* about which he said, *'he will be given an easy reckoning'* (84:8); *'and some outdo each other in good by*

1. Ahmad related it in the *Musnad* 2/163. According to al-Arna'ud, the *isnad* is weak. Its men are reliable men of the *Sahih* except for Abu'z-Zubayr whose personal name is Muhammad ibn Muslim ibn Tadris: he did not hear *hadiths* from 'Abdullah ibn 'Umar, according to what Abu Hatim said in *al-Marasil.*

2. Ahmad related it in the Musnad, 4/299, According to al-Arna'ud, its *isnad* is sound and its men are reliable.

Allah's permission.' about which he said, 'They are those who will enter the Garden without reckoning.'"[1]

Al-Bara' ﷺ said, "The Prophet ﷺ instructed us to do seven things and forbade us seven. He instructed us to join funeral processions, visit the sick, accept invitations, help the wronged, fulfil our oaths, return greetings, and bless people who sneeze. He forbade us silver vessels, gold rings, silk, silk brocade, *qissi* silk and *istabraq* silk." [al-Bukhari, 1172]

Ibn 'Abbas ﷺ related that the Messenger of Allah ﷺ said to Mu'adh ibn Jabal when he sent him to the Yemen, "You are going to a people who have Scripture. When you come to them, call on them to testify that there is no god but Allah and that Muhammad is the Messenger of Allah. When they obey you in respect of that, then tell them that Allah has made five prayers obligatory for them in each twenty-four day. When they obey you in respect of that, inform them that Allah has made it obligatory for *zakat* to be taken from their property and given to their poor. If they obey you in respect of that, beware of the precious things of people and beware of the supplication of someone wronged. There is no screen between him and Allah." (al-Bukhari, 1425)

Zayd ibn Aslam related from his father ﷺ that 'Umar ibn al-Khattab ﷺ appointed a client of his called Hunayy over the *hima* preserve. He said, "Hunayy! Be gentle to the Muslims and fear the supplication of the wronged, for the supplication of the wronged is answered. Let the one who has few camels and the owner of sheep enter. Beware of the herds of Ibn 'Awf and the herds of Ibn 'Affan. Even if their livestock were to die, they could resort to palm-trees and crops. If someone who has few camels and an owner of sheep were to have their flocks perish, they would bring their sons to me and say, 'O Amir al-Mu'minin!' Could I neglect them? No, may you be fatherless! So water and herbage are easier for me to grant than gold and silver. By Allah, they think that I have wronged them. This is their

1. Ahmad related it in the *Musnad* 5/194). According to al-Arna'ud, that its *isnad* is weak.

land, and they fought for it in the *Jahiliyya;* and when they became Muslim they possessed it. By the One in whose hand my soul is, were it not for the animals which I provide to be ridden in the way of Allah, I would not have made a handspan of their land into a preserve." [al-Bukhari 2894]

'Abdullah ibn Sarjis ﷺ said, "When the Messenger of Allah ﷺ travelled, he sought refuge from the hardship of the journey, from a sorrowful return, from decrease after wealth, and from the supplication of the wronged, and from any evil sight in respect of his family or property."[1]

Abu Hurayra ﷺ said that the Prophet ﷺ said, "Three supplications will be answered without a doubt: the supplication of a parent, the supplication of a traveller, and the supplication of someone who is wronged."[2]

Abu Hurayra related that the Messenger of Allah ﷺ said, "Three do not have their supplication rejected: a just imam, someone fasting until he breaks his fast, and the supplication of someone who is wronged is raised above the clouds and the gates of heaven open for it, And the Almighty Lord says, 'By My might, I will help you, even if it is after some time.'"[3]

Al-Bara' related that the Messenger of Allah ﷺ passed by some of the Ansar who were sitting in the road and said, "If you must do that, then return greetings, help the wronged and guide the traveller."[4]

'Abdullah ibn Sarjis ﷺ said, "When the Prophet ﷺ set out on a journey, he used to say, ' O Allah, You are our Companion on the journey and our Deputy in our family. O Allah, I seek refuge with You from the hardship of this journey and an unfortunate return. O Allah, accompany us in our journey and stand in for us in our family. (I seek refuge from) from decrease after wealth, from the supplication of the wronged, and from and from any evil sight in respect of my family or property.'"[5]

1. Al-Bukhari, 1343.
2. Abu Dawud, 1536. Al-Albani said that it is *hasan.*
3. Al-Tirmidhi, 2526. Al-Albani says that it is sound.
4. At-Tirmidhi, 2726. Al-Albani said that its text is sound.
5. At-Tirnidhi, 3439, Al-Albani says that it is sound.

Abu Hurayra ﷺ said that the Messenger of Allah ﷺ said, "O son of Adam, act as if you could (truly) see, count yourself among the dead, and beware of the supplication of the wronged."[1]

Abu Hurayra ﷺ said that the Messenger of Allah ﷺ said, "The supplication of the one who has been wronged is anwered. If he is impious, his impiety is against him."[2]

Anas ibn Malik ﷺ said that the Messenger of Allah ﷺ said, "Fear the supplication of the wronged person, even if he is an unbeliever. There is no veil over it."[3]

It is related from Abu'sh-Shammakh al-Azdi from a nephew of his who was one of the Companions of the Prophet ﷺ, that he went to Mu'awiya, entered his presence, and said, "I heard the Messenger of Allah ﷺ say, 'If someone is put in charge of the business of the people and then closes his door to the poor, the wronged or someone with a need, Allah Almighty will close the doors of His mercy to him when he is poor and in need and is in greater need of it.'"[4]

It is related that al-Bara' ﷺ said, "The Messenger of Allah ﷺ passed by some people sitting in the road and said, 'If you must do that, then guide the traveller, return greetings, and assist the wronged."

'Affan said, "Help the wronged."[5]

1. Ahmad related it in the *Musnad*, 2/343. Al-Arna'ut says that the *hadith* can be considered *hasan* but its *isnad* is weak.

2. Ahmad related it in the *Musnad*, 2/367. Al-Arna'ut said that its *isnad* is weak.

3. Ahmad related it in the *Musnad*, 2/153. Al-Arna'ut said that its *isnad* is weak.

4. Ahmad related it in the *Musnad*, 3/480. Al-Arna'ut said that others consider it sound.

5. Ahmad related it in the *Musnad* 4/2910. Al-Arna'ut said that it is a sound *hadith* whose transmitters are reliable. The variant of at-Tirmidhi has already been mentioned.

7. The Greatest Wrongdoing and Injustice

'Abdullah said, "When *'Those who believe and do not mix their belief with any wrongdoing'* (4:82) was revealed, the Companions of the Messenger of Allah ﷺ said, 'Which of us does not do wrong?' Then Allah revealed, *'Attributing partners to Him is a terrible wrong.'* (31:13)"[1]

In one version reported from him, he said, "When *'Those who believe and do not mix their belief with any wrongdoing,'* (4:82) was revealed, we asked, 'Messenger of Allah, which of us does not do wrong?' he replied, 'It is not as you say. *"Do not mix their belief with any wrongdoing"* means "with *shirk*". Have you not heard what Luqman told his son? *"O my son, do not associate anything with Allah. Attributing partners to Him is a terrible wrong."*(31:13)'"[2]

In another version from him, he said, "When *'Those who believe and do not mix their belief with any wrongdoing,'* (4:82) was revealed, that was hard on the Companions of the Messenger of Allah ﷺ and they asked, 'Which of us does not wrong himself?' The Messenger of Allah ﷺ replied, 'It is not as you suppose. It is as Luqman told his son, *"O my son, do not associate anything with Allah. Attributing partners to Him is a terrible wrong."* (31:13)'"

Al-Hafiz Ibn Hajar said in *Fath al-Bari*, "The words of 'Abdullah ibn Mas'ud ﷺ: 'When *"Those who believe and do not mix their belief with any wrongdoing,"* (4:82) was revealed, it was hard on the Companions of the Messenger of Allah, may Allah bless him and grant him peace, and they asked, 'Which of us does not wrong himself?' The Messenger of Allah ﷺ replied, 'It is not as you suppose. It is as Luqman told his son, *"O my son, do not associate anything with Allah. Attributing partners to Him is a terrible wrong."* (31:13)'"

This is how the *hadith* occurs in the *Sahih Muslim*. In the *Sahih al-Bukhari* it occurs as: "When the *ayat* was revealed, the Companions of the Messenger of Allah ﷺ asked, 'Which of us does not do wrong?' Then Allah revealed, *'Attributing partners to*

1. Al-Bukhari, 32 and Muslim 197/124.
2. Al-Bukhari, *al-Jami' as-Sahih* (3181).

Him is a terrible wrong.' (31:13)" These two transmissions explain one another. So when that was hard on them, Allah Almighty revealed, *"Attributing partners to Him is a terrible wrong."*

According to an-Nawawi, "The Prophet ﷺ informed us that the normally unqualified term 'wrongdoing' is here qualified and means *shirk*. The Prophet ﷺ said to his Companions after that, 'It does not mean wrongdoing in a general and unqualified way as you supposed. It means *shirk* as Luqman told his son.' The Companions, may Allah be pleased with them, took the word 'wrongdoing' in its general meaning and were too hasty in understanding it, thus putting something in what was not its proper place. That is contrary to the *Shari'a*, and so it was hard on them until the Prophet ﷺ informed them about what was actually meant by wrongdoing in this instance."

Al-Khattabi said, "It was hard on them because the apparent meaning of wrongdoing is acting contrary to the rights of people and that by which they wrong themselves through committing disobedience. They thought that what was meant was the literal meaning. The basic meaning of 'wrongdoing' (*zulm*) is to put a thing in what is not its proper place. So someone who assigns worship to other than Allah Almighty is the most unjust of the unjust. This *hadith* also informs us that disobedience is not unbelief. Allah knows best."

It is reported from 'Abdullah ibn 'Umar ﷺ that the Prophet ﷺ said, "Injustice will be darkness on the Day of Rising."[1]

Ibn al-Jawzi said, "There are two categories of injustice: taking someone else's wealth without right, and opposing the Lord. Disobeying Him in that regard is worse than any other wrongdoing because other injustice is normally only inflicted on someone weak and unable to defend himself. Injustice is engendered by darkness of heart because if someone's heart had been illuminated by the light of guidance, he would have reflected and acted differently. While those who are godfearing strive by their light which they receive because of their fear of Allah, a wrongdoer is

1. Al-Bukhari 2315 and Muslim 57/2579.

encompassed by the darkness of wrongdoing so that nothing can help him at all against his wrongdoing."

"'Abdullah ibn 'Umar ﷺ reported that the Messenger of Allah ﷺ said, "The Muslim is the brother of the Muslim. He should not wrong him or hand him over to his enemy.'"[1]

Al-Hafiz Ibn Hajar said, "The words 'he should not wrong him' are in the past tense which here has the meaning of a command, meaning that it is forbidden for a Muslim to wrong another Muslim. The words, 'he should not surrender him' mean that he must not leave him with someone who will harm him or in a situation which will be harmful for him. Rather he should help him and defend him. This is more specific than refraining from wrongdoing. That may be either mandatory or recommended according to different circumstances." At-Tabarani added by another chain of narration from Salim, 'He does not leave him in any calamity that may befall him.'"

Muslim states in the *hadith* related from Abu Hurayra: "He should not disdain him,' that it means: "It is enough evil for a man that he should disdain his Muslim brother."[2]

Anas ibn Malik ﷺ used to state that the Messenger of Allah ﷺ said, "Help your brother, wronging or wronged." A man asked, "Messenger of Allah, I can help someone wronged, but how do him if he is wronging?" He answered, "You restrain him from wronging. That is helping him."[3]

In another variant, "He takes hold of his hands."[4]

8. This Book

The pages of this book contain some of the thoughts of Shaykh Imam Muhammad Mitwalli ash-Sha'rani about injustice and those who are unjust. We prepared his material and made a commentary and notes on it and traced the source of its *hadith*s

1. Al-Bukhari 2310 and Muslim 58/2580.
2. Part of a *hadith* transmitted by Muslim, 32/2564.
3. Al-Bukhari 6552 and Muslim 62/2584 has the like. It already has been recited above in a *hadith* of at-Tirmidhi.
4. Al-Bukhari 2312.

and added similar material by the other scholars. I prepared it with care, traced *hadith*s and then added notes to make it more useful.

We ask Allah Almighty to benefit its reader, writer and publisher. May the Shaykh be given the best reward from us and light in his grave and raised up a degree among the guided; and may Allah place him with the Prophets, the truthful, the martyrs and the righteous. Allah – glory be to Him – is All-Hearing, Near, Answering.

O Allah, bless and grant peace to our master Muhammad, and his family and Companions.

Praise be to Allah, the Lord of the Worlds.

'Abdullah Hajjaj

Jumada al-Akhir 1422
August 2002

Injustice and the Unjust
Shaykh Muhammad ash-Sha'rawi

Injustice

Imam Muhammad Mitwalli ash-Sha'rawi said: Praise be to Allah, the Lord of the worlds; blessings and peace be upon the best of the Messengers, the Seal of the Prophets and the mercy of Allah upon the universe, our master Muhammad, the "ear of good" who received the last message of heaven for the guidance of the earth, and "the tongue of truthfulness" who conveyed what Allah desired for His creation; and on his family and Companions, who called to truth and were the masters of creation.

Allah ﷻ says: *"We destroyed generations before you when they did wrong. Their Messengers brought them the Clear Signs, but they were never going to believe. That is how We repay evil-doers."* (10:13)

Beware of allowing your lower selves to entice you into doing wrong by your aggression against Muhammad ﷺ because you will not succeed in any of it. Allah will perfect His light and you are no different from previous peoples.

The Arabic word for "generations" (qurūn) is the plural of *qarn* which is related to the word muqarāna, meaning "comparison". Every group which is interconnected in some way we call a generation or *qarn.* This connectedness may be in terms of time which is why the word is sometimes used as a synonym for a century. The people who are included within a period of a hundred years are called a generation. A *qarn* can be a group who are connected by something which groups them together, no matter how long the time actually is.

Allah says, *"We destroyed generations before you when they did wrong. Their Messengers brought them the Clear Signs, but they were never going to believe."* If Allah Almighty were to reprieve them, would they then believe? No. Allah has pre-eternal knowledge. He knows things according to what will transpire, whether that be by necessity or choice. An example from our own lives can be found in people who want to build a house. The project inevitably varies according to capacity. A poor man, for instance, will merely want to build two rooms, and makes a simple plan to accord with his intention of building two rooms. If a man is of middling wealth, he goes to an architect who will design a house for him according to his wealth. If a man is rich, he invites an architect to design him a house according to his desires and gives the engineer a clear outline before he begins, showing every detail, even down to the colours of the window frames, doors and rooms.

When Allah ﷻ created the world, its form had already been determined before time with Him. This is absolute power which belongs to Allah Almighty. He brought about actual being according to what He had previously determined for it. Even if there is a choice for an unbelieving being, Allah knows it. It is true to say that the ink has dried even concerning matters of choice. Allah knows what compulsory matters will be and what He has decided for His creation without any choice on their part. As for voluntary matters, He has given creatures choice but He knows what they will do in the Unseen and the matter is determined according to what He knows.

Beware of thinking that that means that He forces you into a particular choice. No, He simply knows in advance what you will choose. That is how Allah ﷻ knows those who will wrong themselves – 'before-time' – as He already knew that He would destroy the people of past generations who did not believe.

"We destroyed generations before you when they did wrong." The meaning of wrongdoing or injustice is to usurp someone's right and give it to someone else. Rights are given by the Creator to mankind and they wrong one another in respect of them. The highest degree of injustice, however, is *shirk*. Allah Almighty says, *"Attributing partners to Him is a terrible wrong."* (31:13) When someone wrongs himself, he puts another god together

with Allah. So that is the pinnacle of injustice, and that is why the Almighty said, *"Attributing partners to Him is a terrible wrong."* So people do wrong by adopting an inappropriate creed or do wrong in respect of the rights they owe one another, thus confirming the words of Allah, *"Rather it is people who wrong themselves."* (10:44)

A person can be wronging and wronged at the same time, since man has many natural aptitudes. Among these are the aptitude for natural faith and the aptitude for immediate self-interest. When the aptitude for immediate self-interest dominates, the critical self emerges to return a person to what is correct. If the self which commands evil appears, it will only seek to realise its lower appetites because that is the nature of a self which commands to evil. However, if it is a self which is at peace with the decree of Allah Almighty and pleased with it and performs what Allah Almighty has instructed, then it is truly a soul at peace. Whoever wrongs himself follows the lower appetites of his self. He gives it the immediate enjoyment it demands, the result of which will be that it will later meet misery, and so by doing that he has truly wronged himself.

"We destroyed generations before you when they did wrong. Their Messengers brought them the Clear Signs". Allah Almighty is the Highest Knower who knows things according to what will be, not according to what He compels His creation to do. If His knowledge had been according to what creation is compelled to do, it would be limited.

An example illustrating this is that of being in a house and wanting to go on a journey with your wife. If your children are small, you lock the door after telling them, "There is food for you in the refrigerator: meat, fish, cheese and olives." After you have gone out, your wife says, "Our children will only eat the cheese and olives because they will find that easier." If there had only been cheese in the refrigerator she would not have said that because then they would have had no choice, whereas as things are they do have real choice in the matter. However, you know in advance how children behave, and when you return you sure enough find that your children acted as you thought they would even though you left them a real choice of doing otherwise.

An example of this in the Qur'an is the words of Allah ﷻ, *"Ruin to the hands of Abu Lahab and ruin to him! His wealth has not helped him nor anything he has earned. He will burn in a Flaming Fire."* (111:1-3) In this is a judgement from Allah Almighty that Abu Lahab would die an unbeliever like other unbelievers. Yet many unbelievers came to believe. Did not 'Umar become Muslim? Did not 'Ikrima, the son of Abu Lahab, become Muslim? Did not 'Amr ibn al-'As become Muslim? Did not Khalid ibn al-Walid become Muslim? Was there anything to prevent Abu Lahab from becoming Muslim in the end! No. But he did not become Muslim, and the Messenger of Allah ﷺ knew from his Lord that that would be the case. It was not even possible for Abu Lahab to practise deception and announce that he was a Muslim in order to deny the Qur'an, because Allah knew before time how he would behave.

"We destroyed generations before you when they did wrong. Their Messengers brought them the Clear Signs, but they were never going to believe. That is how We repay evil-doers." (10:13) His words, *"That is how"* means: the like of this repayment by which the previous generations were destroyed in past generations will be how Allah will repay any present or future human beings who act in the same way. The repayment comes from the One who defines everything because the cases in existence are the same. The case of faith has existed from the first of the Messengers sent and will exist until the end of the world.

Allah does not wrong by even the weight of an atom

Allah Almighty says, *"That is on account of what you did. Allah does not wrong His slaves."* (3:182)

The word for "wrongdoer" (ẓallām) used here is an intensive form denoting someone who commits a great amount of wrongdoing or injustice. Someone who eats normally is called "ākil" but someone who is called "akkāl" is a glutton, someone who eats great deal. The intensive form stresses the action of taking food. In the same way, you call person nājir when you want to indicate someone who just takes a piece of wood without any particular expertise and does something with it. If, however, you call someone najjār, using the intensive form, you mean that he is a carpenter and working with wood is his craft. The same is true of khā'iṭ which means someone who sews something and khayyāṭ which means tailor. Likewise if you say that someone is jāzir that means he is able to slaughter but if you call someone jazzār, it means he is a butcher whose work is slaughtering.

So the form fa''āl is an intensive nominal form and there are two cases where this intensive form is used. One is for affirmation and one is for denial. When you say, "So-and-so is a glutton (akkāl), you confirm that he has the intensive form of eating. Therefore the basic attribute of eating itself is taken for granted. As long as it is confirmed that he has the intensive form of the attribute, the basic attribute is confirmed absolutely. If you say, "So-and-so is a tailor (khayyāṭ)," you confirm that he knows how to sew. If you call him carpenter (najjār) you confirm that he knows how to work in wood.

As for the negative aspect, when you say that someone is not a glutton, this is a negation of the intensive form, but it does not negate the fact that he eats. When you say that someone is not a carpenter, you deny that he has expertise in carpentry, but you do not deny that he works with wood. If you say that so-and-so is not highly erudite ('allāma), he may still be a scholar ('ālim). When you confirm the intensive you also confirm the basic. When you negate the intensive you do not necessarily negate the basic. When you say, 'So-and-so is not a wrongdoer (ẓallām)," you deny their intensive wrongdoing but leave open the possibility that they still commit some wrong; they may be only ẓālim and not ẓallām. So the words "He is not ẓallām" negate the excessive form only, but does not negate the fact of wrongdoing (ẓulm) itself.

It is extraordinary that the orientalists say that the *ayat*s of Qur'an contradict one another. For instance, in the *ayat* quoted above Allah ﷻ, says, *"He does not wrong (*ẓallām*)"* (3:182), negating the intensive, and, as we have seen, the negation of the intensive does not necessarily mean the negation of the basic, and then He says in another *ayat*, *"Allah does not wrong anyone by so much as the smallest mote."* (4:40) negating both the intensive and the basic forms of wrongdoing. They say that this is contradiction. We say: "Does the negation of the intensive mean that the basic attribute is necessarily affirmed?" Of course not. The negation of the intensive does not preclude the existence of the basic but it does not necessitate its existence either.

So the words of Allah ﷻ, *"Allah does not wrong anyone by so much as the smallest mote"* (4:40), negate any wrongdoing whatsoever; and the words of the Almighty, *"Allah does not wrong His slaves"* (3:182), negate the principle of excess. The Qur'an explains itself. When it is said that Allah negates the intensive and this implies confirmation of the basic attribute, we say that the negation of the intensive does not necessitate the basic; it merely does not preclude its existence. Then another *ayat* comes and negates the basic attribute itself, and so Allah is shown not to be unjust in any way – neither ẓallām nor ẓālim.

We must turn to the inimitability of the Qur'an in respect of its use of language. The speaker is Allah and every word counts. He says *"Allah does not wrong His slaves"*, and so we must pay attention to the fact that the intensive form is used here. If you say that someone is a glutton, using the intensive form of "eat", you indicate that he eats excessively, but you do not say in what way. For instance a glutton may eat five loaves in one meal or a glutton may eat a reasonable amount of food at any one time, but eat it ten times a day. So the excessive can manifest itself in the strength of a particular occurrence – even if the action does not recur – or it may manifest itself in the repetition of a particular action. If a human being commits extensive wrongdoing on a particular occasion, he is called ẓallām because he goes to excess in wrongdoing at that time. If, however, someone is not excessive in their wrongdoing – their wrongdoing may even be comparatively slight – but it involves a large number of people, he is called ẓallām because of the number of people wronged.

Allah ﷻ says, "Allah does not wrong His *slaves.*" He does not say, "He does not wrong His *slave.*" Since wrongdoing is commensurate with ability, the ability of a ruler to do injustice is greater than the power of someone with limited influence; but even someone of limited influence has more power than a normal person. So if Allah ﷻ were to do wrong to each of His slaves – far be it from Him! – even by the amount of a mote, one would have to use the form "ẓallām". Thus by this noble *ayat* Allah ﷻ means to tell us that He does not wrong anyone, even by the weight of an atom. For if He had wronged every one of His slaves by even so insignificant an amount as the weight of an atom, the amount of the injustice would be stupendous because of the vast number of slaves involved; but not even this amount of injustice occurs in respect of Allah ﷻ because "*Allah does not wrong His slaves.*"

The Messenger, may Allah bless him and grant him peace, is free of wrongdoing or injustice

Az-Zubayr ibn al-'Awwam, may Allah be pleased with him – and he was one of the ten who were promised the Garden and was the son of the paternal aunt of the Messenger of Allah ﷺ – had a disagreement with one of the Ansar about watering some land of his in al-Harra, which is a place close to Madina. Its land is smooth and covered with black stones. They took the dispute to the Messenger of Allah ﷺ, and the Messenger of Allah ﷺ said to az-Zubayr, "Irrigate, Zubayr, and then let the water pass through to your neighbour." It would not have been logical for the Messenger of Allah ﷺ to wrong his cousin, and no one could say that he had given judgement in his favour either.

The Messenger of Allah ﷺ was far removed from giving any unjust judgement: he was famous for his justice. Some people act like this out of a desire for fame. With this sort of person, if one of their children has a disagreement with someone, they will give judgement in favour of the stranger rather than the child. We say to this sort of person, "Do not make an unjust ruling in order to be famous for justice among people. There is a kind of courage which you should possess: that is, the courage to give a fair judgement. Courage demands that you judge in favour of what is right, even if it is for yourself."

When, however, the Prophet ﷺ ruled in favour of his cousin, az-Zubayr, the Ansari did not like that. He said to the Messenger of Allah ﷺ, "He is your aunt's son." Sometimes the Arabs say something elliptically and leave the rest for the listener to understand. The face of the Messenger of Allah ﷺ changed colour and then he said, "Irrigate, Zubayr, and then retain the water until it reaches the level of the wall." Several people who want to catch out Islam say, "The Messenger of Allah ﷺ first judged that his cousin could water but then changed the judgement regarding the water for the Ansari."

They do not understand that the land of az-Zubayr was higher than the land of Hatib, the Ansari, which was lower down. When we look at fertile locations, we find them at the bottom of valleys – not at the feet of mountains – because although water starts at higher ground it always flows to the lower place. Therefore if we were to water the lower land first, this would be unfair to the higher land.[1] So the first ruling was based on making things easy and was a favour on the part of az-Zubayr to the Ansari, whereas the other judgement was based on strict fairness.[2]

1. That is what Imam al-Bukhari believed in his interpretation of the *hadith*, 5/312. *Fath,* when he headed it, "Chapter: Watering the upper part before the lower."

2. Al-Bukhari transmitted the *hadith*, 2359, *Fath*: also in Muslim, 129/2357, Abu Dawud, 336, and at-Tirmidhi 1363 from 'Abdullah ibn az-Zubayr ﵁.

An-Nawawi discussed this *hadith*, "After the words of the Prophet ﷺ, 'Irrigate Zubayr, and then let the water pass through to your neighbour,' the Ansari became angry and said, 'Messenger of Allah, is it because he is your cousin?' The face of the Prophet of Allah ﷺ changed colour and then he said, 'Irrigate, Zubayr, and then retain the water until it reaches the level of the wall.' The words, 'Is it because he is your cousin?' imply 'You have done this because he is your cousin.' The words 'His face changed colour' mean that it changed because of the anger felt at the man's violation of the respect due to Prophethood, and at the ugliness of his words.

Jadr or *jidr* means wall (jidâr*)*. 'Reaches the level of the wall' means that the water rises to it. 'Wall' here means the foundation of the wall. It is also said to refer to the roots of trees. The sound position is the first one. Scholars estimate that level to be reached when the water rises above all of the ground concerned until it wets a man's ankles. The owner of the first land which is next to the water retains the water on his land until it reaches this level and then lets it pass through to his neighbour after him. Az-Zubayr owned the first land and the Messenger of Allah ﷺ, knowing about that, said, 'Irrigate and then let the water pass through to your neighbour,' meaning, 'Take a little water, which is less than your full right, and then let it pass through to your neighbour,' being confident that az-Zubayr would be content with that and prefer doing good to his neighbour. When the neighbour said what he said, the Prophet ﷺ commanded him to take his full right."

The explanation of this *hadith* has already been made clear in this chapter. If the like of these words spoken by the Ansari ascribing bias to the Prophet were to issue today from someone, it would constitute unbelief and the judgements due to an apostate would have to be carried out on the one who said it. It would be mandatory to execute him provided the necessary preconditions had been met. The Prophet ﷺ did not do this because it, was at the beginning of Islam when people were becoming familiar with it and so his restraint represents repelling evil with what is better and being patient in face of the harm of "the hypocrites and those in whose heart there was illness".

He used to say, "Make things easy and do not make them difficult. Give good news and do not make people averse." He said, "People will not say that Muhammad kills his Companions." Allah says, *"You will never cease to come upon some act of treachery on their part, except for a few of them. Yet pardon them, and overlook. Allah loves good-doers."* (5:13) Ad-Dawudi related that this man who argued with az-Zubayr was a hypocrite. The words in the *hadith* stating that he was an Ansari do not contradict this because he was one of their tribe, not one of the Muslim Ansar.

The words at the end of the *hadith*, "He said to az-Zubayr, 'By Allah, I reckon that this *ayat* was revealed about it: *"No, by your Lord, they are not believers until they make you their judge in the disputes that break out between them, and then find no resistance within and submit themselves completely."* (4:65)'" lead one school of thought to say that this incident was the reason for its revelation.

Injustice towards the self

Injustice towards the lower self occurs when a human being satisfies his immediate appetites in a way that will result in his own enduring wretchedness. So the human being is in the position of an exile who should not gratify all the appetites of his lower self because the gratification of immediate appetites is liable to bring him abiding misery. Injustice to the lower self is the most wretched of all types of injustice. Can anyone be said to be truly intelligent who disobeys Allah by neglecting His commands and accepting things which He has forbidden?

An intelligent person will not do so, because he recognises that while the outward appearance of the business is the satisfaction of an appetite, the inward reality of the business is immersion in misery. The command is to pray. If a man is lazy and sleeps through the prayer, in the outward that gives him the pleasure of sleep, but in the inward it brings about separation from Allah. The command is not to drink wine. If a human being does not abide by that and drinks, he thinks that he has achieved pleasure for himself, but the reality of the matter is that he has wronged himself because that will bring about great misery. When a human being wrongs himself, he is not a proper trustee over his own affairs.

Justice demands both a wronger and wronged, so what is the state of someone who commits wrong against himself? Who is the wronger? Who is the wronged? The term *nafs* or "self" is applied to the joining of the rūḥ or spirit to the substance of the body. This can result in three different states: a self which has

---

It is said that it was revealed about two men who went to the Prophet ﷺ for judgement, and that he gave judgement against one of them who said, 'Present the case to 'Umar ibn al-Khattab.'

It is said that it was about a Jew and a hypocrite who took a dispute to the Prophet ﷺ, and the hypocrite was not content with his judgement and asked for a soothsayer to judge it.

Ibn Jarir said, "It is possible that it was revealed about all of that. Allah Almighty knows best." The Prophet ﷺ said, "Avoid what I forbid you and do what I command you as much as possible."

the attribute of being at peace; a self which has the attribute of commanding evil; or a self which has the attribute of being self-critical. As soon as the rūḥ is combined with matter, the human self comes into being. Before the rūḥ joined bodily matter, it was by its nature good, and before the rūḥ joined it, bodily matter was by its nature good.

I say this so that no one can say that there is material life and spiritual life and that material life is evil but spiritual life is good. That is because matter in general is good and obeys and worships and glorifies Allah; and the same applies to the spirit. Corruption develops at the moment when spirit is cast into matter. When they meet and interaction comes about, then freedom of choice comes into play and the human being, who is accountable for his actions, is asked, "Are you content with the judgement of Allah? Do you vacillate between self-criticism and being at peace? Or are you drowned in disobedience so that your self commands you to do evil?" This disagreement arises when the spirit joins with matter.

When the spirit meets the substance of the body, who wrongs whom? Passion which opposes Allah is what wrongs the self. The one who errs in the outward matter satisfies the appetite of his lower self by opposing Allah, but the truth of the matter is that he is wronging himself. That is why Allah Almighty says, *"If only when they wronged themselves..."* (4:64) There is a difference between a man committing an outrageous act satisfy his own desires and a man committing an outrageous act to satisfy someone else's desires. Allah says about that, *"Those who, when they act indecently or wrong themselves, remember Allah and ask forgiveness for their bad actions – and who can forgive bad actions except Allah?"* (3:135)

That is how we recognise that outrageous actions are one thing and wronging the self is another. Doing an outrageous action may give the self enjoyment for a moment. The one who wrongs himself in order to satisfy someone else's desire does not give himself any enjoyment but still wrongs himself. He neither gives himself the enjoyment of the moment in this world nor does he protect himself from punishment in the Next World. An example of that is a perjurer who testifies so that the right of another man can be unfairly taken away. What does this witness obtain? He obtains nothing but wronging himself. That is why it is related: "The worst of you is the one who sells his *deen* in exchange for this world, and still worse still than him is the one who sells his *deen* for the worldly portion of someone else."[1]

This is the injustice of the bad self. They are also those whose efforts in the life of this world have gone astray while they reckon that they are doing good."[2]

1. I have not been able to find the source of this in any of the references I have.

2. Allah Almighty says, *"Say: 'Shall I inform you of the greatest losers in their actions? People whose efforts in the life of this world are misguided while they suppose that they are doing good.'"* (18:103-104) Mus'ab ﷺ said, "I asked my father (i.e. Sa'd ibn Abi Waqqas) about the words of Allah, *'Say: "Shall I inform you of the greatest losers in their actions?"'* and whether it referred to the Haruriyya (the Kharijites). He answered, 'No, it is about the Jews and the Christians. The Jews denied Muhammad ﷺ and the Christians denied the Garden and said, "There is no food or drink in it." The Haruriyya broke the contract of Allah after it had been made.' Sa'd ﷺ called them *fasiqun* (deviants).'"

'Ali ibn Abi Talib, ad-Dahhak and several others said that the people meant are the Haruriyya. This meaning is reported from 'Ali ﷺ who said that this noble *ayat* includes the Haruriyya just as it also refers to the Jews and Christians and others, since it was not revealed about either the former or the latter: it is more general. This *ayat* is Makkan before the Jews and Christians were addressed and before the Kharijites even existed. It is general to all who worship in a manner which is not pleasing and who suppose that they are correct in what they do and that their actions are accepted, while in fact they are in error and their actions rejected – as the Almighty says, *"Some faces on that Day will be downcast, labouring, toiling endlessly, roasting in a red-hot Fire."* (88:2-4) The Almighty also says, *"We will advance on the actions they have done and make them scattered specks of dust"* (25:23), and the Almighty says, *"But the actions of those who reject are like a mirage in the desert. A thirsty man thinks it water but when he reaches it, he finds it nothing at all."* (24:29) He says in this noble *ayat*, *"Say: 'Shall I inform you?'"*, i.e. tell you *"of the greatest losers"*. Then He explains it by saying, *"People whose efforts in the life of this world are misguided,"* meaning that they did false actions which are outside the prescribed, pleasing, and accepted *Shari'a*. *"While they suppose that they are doing good"* means they believe that they have something good and that they are accepted and loved.

Injustice is like tyranny, which is a type of transgression using coercion and force that detracts from the power or value of others. The opposite of injustice is fairness, as justice is the opposite of tyranny. Injustice, then, entails diminishing another's right, so what do you think about the case when a human being decreases his own right – in other words, wrongs himself so that he is wronged by his own self? Wronging one's self is the most horrible form of injustice. The self which Allah has created and with which Allah has honoured him is entitled to respect from the human being who houses it; and he should realise what Allah desires of it and deny it its insistent desire for what will anger Allah. It is the injustice of the self which the Almighty is talking about when He says, "*Those who, when they act indecently or wrong themselves, remember Allah and ask forgiveness for their bad actions – and who can forgive bad actions except Allah? – and do not knowingly persist in what they were doing. Their recompense is forgiveness from their Lord, and Gardens with rivers flowing under them, remaining in them timelessly, forever. How excellent is the reward of those who act!*" (3:135-136)

We find that injustice to the self can consist of another sort of bad action as well. Injustice to the self means that a man sells his *deen* for the worldly portion of someone else. Someone who does this does not achieve any benefit for himself, either sooner or later.

The first kind is that about which it is said, "The worst of people is the one who sells his *deen* for this world." They are those who commit outrageous actions. The second kind is that about which it is said, "Worse are those who sell their *deen* for the worldly portion of another." Allah has prescribed for both types a means of salvation through remembering Allah and asking forgiveness and not returning to the like of those outrageous actions or wronging the self, so that Allah may forgive them and admit them into the Garden. That is because Allah does not wrong anyone. *"Rather it is people who wrong themselves."* (10:44) Why? Because people curtail their own right to what is beneficial and lasting and become captives to what vanishes.

So we find that a human being may be both wronging and wronged at the same time, that is because people wrong themselves. The human self has faculties directed to immediate benefit, faculties of appetite, and so on. These faculties contend with one another. If you do evil and then you blame yourself for doing it, then you do good and you have a self-critical self. If your self has an uncontrolled natural tendency for evil and appetite, you have a self which commands to evil. If your self is at peace with Allah Almighty, then you have a self which is at peace.

The self which commands evil is the one which usurps the rights of other people and wrongs them, but at the same time, you wrong yourself by giving in to its desire for immediate gratification and leading it to lasting wretchedness.

Forbidding reliance on the unjust

Allah Almighty says, *"Do not rely on those who do wrong."* (11:113) Relying includes feeling inclination, satisfaction, love and mercy towards something. The reason for His words, *"Do not rely on those who do wrong"* is that if you rely on a wrongdoer – in other words, incline towards him and make him a friend – Allah will include you with him; but if you are far from him and do not rely on him, you have taken refuge with a strong pillar. Do not rely on him. Then he will understand that you are trusting in Allah and in His power against wrongdoers and he will feel weak. The great calamity in this world is that we seek the help of the wrongdoers, and help them in spite of their injustice. Someone who seeks the help of a wrongdoer does not turn to Allah Almighty who is able to sweep away this wrongdoer along with all the tyranny, force and power that he wields. Allah Almighty warns us against that and says, *"Do not rely on those who do wrong so that the Fire afflicts you."*

The reason for that is to ensure that we do not assist wrongdoers in their wrongdoing. Rather we should acquaint them with their wrongdoing. If a first time wrongdoer found someone to oppose him he would refrain from his wrongdoing – but what makes him worse is the fact that people aid and abet him in injustice out of fear of him and he finds no one who is able to rise up and oppose him. The worst kind of support a wrongdoer can receive is when he finds people who make his injustice seem attractive to him. This making injustice seem attractive helps to spread injustice. Relying on someone unjust can take many forms. If you were to review all the varieties of injustice in existence, you would find that injustice only spreads because people abet wrongdoers and make their actions seem attractive to them. If they had stood against them from the first, their injustice would not have spread and become worse.

Allah Almighty says, *"You have no protector besides Allah."* (11:113) This means: "You have no protector and no helper except Allah, so do not rely on those who do wrong and do not seek their help. Allah alone is your Helper and Protector." So go straight and follow His commands, and do not leave that for anything else.

Injustice is a reason for destruction

Allah Almighty says, *"How many cities We have destroyed! Our violent force came down on them during the night, or while they were asleep during the day."* (7:4). If the number had been a small one, then the word for "how many", *kam,* would not have been used, so it is clear that the number involved is beyond simple computation. The word *kam* is used when the number is too large to be counted, indicating that it is an uncalculatedly great number. That is how many cities Allah has destroyed on account of their wrongdoing.

The word "city", *qarya,* is a place which is designed in a particular manner so that it contains all the requirements necessary for the livelihood of the people resident in it so that people can find dwellings, food, drink and all that life requires. But does Allah destroy the cities or those who are in the cities? Sometimes He destroys the cities themselves and pulverises them and turns them upside down, as happened to the people of Nuh and the people of Lut. Sometimes He merely destroys the people living in the cities and the Shout seizes them, as happened to the people of Salih.

But what is meant in this *ayat* is the people of the cities. A city comprises buildings and squares, wells and springs, and so forth. All of these things are compelled to obey Allah and glorify Allah Almighty and cannot disobey him. Those who are able to disobey are the people of the town. In the Noble Qur'an Allah Almighty uses the word 'town' as an allusion to its people. He says in *Surat Yusuf*, *"Ask questions of the town in which we were."* (12:82) Naturally, none of the buildings of the town or its earth will be asked. It is the people of the town who will be asked.

But we must turn to the words of Allah Almighty, *"How many cities We have destroyed! Our violent force came down on them during the night, or while they were asleep during the day."* (7:4) Which came first: destruction or force? Force naturally came first and then the people were destroyed. So, according to our knowledge, the *ayat* would seem to mean: "How many a town our force came down on and We destroyed it" because it was the force that destroyed the people. But that is not a true description of what happened, for Allah ﷻ does not want us to understand events by their outward appearance when they occur. We should take them according to what is in the knowledge of Allah ﷻ.

So the destruction of the town did not come about spontaneously, but through a pre-eternal decree from Allah against those who brought about corruption in the earth. Allah decreed first that the city should be destroyed, and then force came to fulfill the command of Allah. So the decree from Allah to destroy them came first, in the knowledge of Allah, before the actual force alighted on them.

How does Allah take revenge on the wrongdoer?

History shows us that. The wrongdoers did a lot to one another. If their true enemies had had power over them, they would have showed mercy to them. It has reached us that our master Malik ibn Dinar, one of the people of good, said, "In some transmissions I saw a *hadith qudsi* in which Allah Almighty says, 'I am the king of Kings and the hearts of kings are in My hand."[1]

Beware of thinking that tyrants, or indeed any rulers or despots, have taken authority through their own intelligence or power. Allah has given it to them in order to discipline wrongdoers. The proof is that sometimes Allah desires to end this situation and, by His majesty, He strips away awe from the hearts of a tyrant's guards and, rather than defending him with their guns, they turn the guns on him.

Beware of thinking that any king has taken his kingdom by force from Allah. Rather when slaves do wrong and transgress, Allah gives power over them to someone who will wrong them. That is why it is said, "The unjust are the sword of Allah on earth by which He takes revenge on others and then Allah in turn takes revenge on them. Allah Almighty says, *"In that way We make the wrongdoers friends of one another because of what they have done."* (6:129)

It is as if the evil imposed on people is the result of their actions. That is why one of the righteous said, "I know my station with my Lord from the character of my mount. When it is headstrong, I say, 'What have I done to make the animal headstrong with me?'" It seemed as if he thought that the matter could be calculated. This is the behaviour of the best of people. When such a person commits a wrong action, he is punished for it immediately so that his page is always clean. The Prophet,

1. al-Hafiz al-Haythami mentioned it in *Majma' az-Zawa'id* as *hadith* no. 9272 from Abu'd-Darda' ﷺ who reported that the Messenger of Allah ﷺ said, "Allah says, 'I am Allah. There is no god but Me, the Master of kings and King of kings. The hearts of kings are in My hand. When the slaves obey Me, the hearts of their kings turn to them with compassion. When slaves disobey, then their hearts turn to them with anger and vengeance and so they make them share in a painful punishment. Do not distract yourselves with supplication against kings, but rather busy yourselves with *dhikr* and simple entreaty. I will protect you against your kings." He said, "At-Tabarani related it in *al-Awsat.* Its chain of transmission contains Wahb ibn Rashid whose narrations are discounted."

peace and blessings be upon him, said, "No disaster strikes a Muslim but that Allah expiates something by it – even a thorn which pricks him."[1]

When one of the people of good does an evil deed, Allah repays him for it by illness in his body or loss in his property. That is what happens to any evildoer whom Allah does not desire to punish in the Next World. The Messenger ﷺ said, "There is no Muslim who is afflicted by illness or anything else but that Allah Almighty removes from him his evil deeds as leaves fall from a tree."[2]

The state of unbelievers and wrongdoers on the Day of Rising

It might occur to the minds of unbelievers that they will be able to ransom themselves from the punishment of the Day of Rising by something. Allah Almighty says, *"If every self that did wrong possessed everything on earth, it would offer it as a ransom."* (10:54) This means that when the unbelievers see the punishment, if they were to possess all the precious things and treasures on the earth, they would offer them all to ransom themselves from the terror that they see. But no compensation or substitute will be accepted from them on that day.

Injustice entails usurping the right of another. The meaning of the right of another is what he earns by legal means. So a wrongdoer comes to what another has earned by his sweat and takes it from him through injustice and transgression. This puts a stop to the movement of life because if, when I work, someone else takes the fruits of my labour, I will stop working.

When a wronger does wrong, he not only takes the right of another, but he leads other strong people to take the rights of the weak and to wrong them, and so injustice spreads. When injustice spreads in a society, then fuility prevails and the whole movement of life comes to a stop. An unjust person takes more

1. Al-Bukhari, 5317 and Muslim 49/2572, from 'A'isha رضي الله عنها.
2. Al-Bukhari (5647) *Fath*, and Muslim 45/2571, from Ibn Mas'ud رضي الله عنه.

than his right, tells lies about others, wrongs them and strips them of their rights. If he were to take all of this world and then come on the Day of Rising wanting to ransom himself from the punishment by all that he has taken, it would not be accepted from him.

This happens because he transgressed, wronged and lied. Allah Almighty says, *"fabricators of lies are bound to fail."* (20:61) This is an outward manifestation in this world before we reach the Next World. Imagine that a man gives bribes, filches and steals. Then after that he falls into the hands of the law. He says to them, "Take what I have and leave me alone." He is just like someone who smuggles a huge amount of foreign money and then, when he is caught, says, "Take all this and let me go." In a moment of temptation, a person commits these wrong actions and evils and is then detained for punishment. He tries to ransom himself by all that he owns, but this will not be accepted in the Next World.

There are two *ayats* of *Surat al-Baqara* which deal with this. The first of them is when Allah ﷻ says, *"Be fearful of a day when no self will be able to compensate for another in any way, nor will any ransom be accepted from it or any intercession benefit it, and they will not be helped."* (2:123) The second *ayat* is the words of the Almighty, *"Show fear of a Day when no self will be able to compensate for another in any way, nor will intercession be accepted from it, nor any ransom taken from it, and they will not be helped."* (2:48)

Those who have an illness in their hearts sometimes try to find in these noble *ayats* a means to sow doubt about the Noble Qur'an. They say that the style is the same and the meaning is the same, but in one case 'ransom' becomes before 'intercession' and in another 'intercession' comes before 'ransom'. In one Allah says, *"no ransom will be **accepted** from it"* and in the other *"no ransom will be **taken** from it"*. Once He says, *"No intercession will be **accepted** from it"* and another time, *"No intercession will **benefit** it."* We say that if those people had truly understood the eloquence of the Arabs, they would have understood that the first *ayat* is eloquent just as the second is eloquent.

The first *ayat* says, *"Be fearful of a day when no self will be able to compensate for another in any way."* How many selves are mentioned? There are two selves. The first self is that which intercedes and the second is the one which is interceded for. The first *ayat* says, *"nor will any ransom be accepted from it"*. This refers to the interceding self first when it attempts to ransom itself by saying, "Take this and let me go free." When that is not accepted from it, it looks for someone else to intercede on its behalf and then that intercession is rejected. That is why the Almighty says in the first *ayat*, *"nor will any ransom be accepted from it or any intercession benefit it..."* (2:123)

In the second *ayat* Allah begins with intercession when someone comes who intercedes with Him on behalf of the wrongdoer, and that intercession is not accepted. When intercession is not accepted, he offers to take on the liability for his companions and this also will be rejected. It will be said, "No ransom will be taken from you." That is why Allah Almighty says in the second *ayat*, *"nor will intercession be accepted from it, nor any ransom taken from it"* (2:48). In other words, in the first *ayat* no ransom is accepted from him and intercession will not help him, and in the second *ayat*, no intercession is accepted nor any ransom taken. That is how we see that the words of the Real *"If every self that did wrong possessed everything on earth, it would offer it as a ransom."* (10:54) mean that if it tried to offer all that is in the earth – if it were to possess that – that ransom would not be accepted from it. If someone else were to intercede for it, his intercession would not be accepted.

Then Allah says, *"They will show their remorse when they see the punishment."* (10:54) "Show" can also mean "conceal". Remorse is regret. Their concealment of it means that it does not show on them. Their hearts are in tatters because the punishment will be immense and make the blood congeal in the veins of the person being punished so that he is unable to cry out. The terror of the Standing will render the tongue dumb and the person will be told, "Speak" but will not be able to speak. Crying out is a sort of physical breathing, and the lack of ability to shout intensifies the torment.

The punishment of wrongdoers in this world before the Next

If all punishment were to be deferred to the Next World then injustice would spread among people. It would worsen throughout all existence. A man who does not believe in the Next World would be free to act antisociably in his life in whatever way he wished. That is why there must be repayment in this world: in order to draw people's attention to the fact Allah ﷻ sustains existence and that the punishment of wrongdoers in this world is a warning and a lesson for others. Then they will return to their Lord and He will punish them severely.

The Almighty says, *"And those who do wrong will have a punishment besides that"* (52:47) – in other words, one that occurs before punishment in the Next World. The Almighty speaks about punishment in this world when He ﷻ says, *"But as for those who deny Our Signs, We will lead them, step by step, into destruction from where they do not know."* (7:182) This means: "We will trick them as an investigator leads on a suspect, asking a question from here and a question from there until his statements contradict themselves and he confesses." Istidrāj (leading on) comes from *daraj*, which is means a stepladder. A stepladder is a means of climbing up from below because it is not possible fom a human to being to climb from the first floor to the fifth in one step, for instance, or to descend from the fifth floor to the first floor.

There must be various steps to allow for the scope of normal movement so that the steps from the high to the low are according to the distance a person is able to move their feet. One aspect of this is that what the foot steps on must be firm, so the movement is achieved by the ability of the body to move without overburdening itself. So the drawing on may be either upwards or downwards. This is in respect of the Next World. The believers are singled out for the highest degrees of the Garden and the unbelievers are singled out for the lowest levels of the Fire. The steps of this world are not like those of the Next World. There is an immense difference.

The meaning of the words of the Real, *"We will lead them on"* applies to this world. It is that Allah draws them on step by step. A lesser punishment comes to them and then He removes it from them and they continue in their disobedience. Then another punishment comes to them and it too is removed from them and so they continue in their transgression. That is how they continue to descend until they reach the punishment of the Fire in the Next World. Allah ﷻ says about that, *"When they forgot what they had been reminded of..."* (6:44) This means that they persist in unbelief and disobedience. *"...We opened up the doors to everything for them,"* meaning, We gave them blessings with respect to health, wealth children and all the blessings of this world.

Then Allah ﷻ says, *"When they were exulting in what they had been given, We suddenly seized them and at once they were in despair."* (6:44) The reason is that when Allah wants to punish a wrongdoing man, He first seizes him gently to give him a chance to desist. If he persists in his transgression, then Allah gives to him until he exults in what he has. Then after that He seizes him with a great force so that he falls from a great height to rock bottom, as happens when a man holds to another in a fight and lifts him up in the air in order to throw him to the ground. Why did he raise him up? So that the fall is all the greater. If he merely threw him down on the ground on which he was standing, the fall would be less severe.

When a human being wants to lead another person on, the person being led often has enough intelligence to be able to avoid the pit into which he is being led. When, however, Allah ﷻ is the One who is leading someone on, no amount of intelligence will be sufficient. That is why Allah ﷻ says, *"We will lead them, step by step, into destruction from where they do not know."* (7:182) This means that the person concerned will not discover that Allah is leading him on so as to be able to save himself, for the simple reason that Allah knows but human beings do not know.

Then Allah ﷻ says, *"I will allow them more time. My subterfuge is sure."* (68:45). Allah ﷻ does not seize the wrongdoer all at once. He takes him step by step until people sense the evils of this wrongdoer; and when Allah seizes him they recognise the value of good, the value of faith and the value of the Path of Allah in a person's life. If every wrongdoer had been seized immediately when he did wrong, people would not be aware of the evils of the wrongdoer and they would not sense the fact that Allah protects them from this wrongdoer and others. The words of Allah ﷻ, *"I will allow them more time"* (68:45) mean "I will grant them a deferral, but I will not neglect them." Here there is only deferment, then after that comes severe seizing. He says, *"My subterfuge is sure."* (68:45)

Subterfuge means plotting. It is secret management against the object of the subterfuge. Strategy can be hidden so that the opponent cannot prepare forces of self-defence in order to repel evil from himself. When human beings plot, their enemies may discover their plotting or they may not. What do you think? When the plotting comes from Allah, will anyone be able to discover it or repel it? Of course this will be impossible. This is why Allah ﷻ says, *"My subterfuge is sure."* The word "sure", matīn, comes from matn, meaning "back". The backbone has to be firm so that it can hold up the body, and it is surrounded by flesh which protects it and strengthens it. The meaning of the words of Allah, *"My subterfuge is sure",* is that it is strong like the pillar that holds up knowledge, which is the strongest thing in it. Matn in *fiqh* consists of succinct words which give us rulings. There must be words of explanation and commentary on these words, but all based on the "text" (*matn*), meaning the strong firm element involved.

Justice – even towards unbelievers and wrongdoers

Allah Almighty says, *"Everything will be decided between them justly. They will not be wronged."* (10:54). How will Allah judge between them when all of them are unbelievers and wrongdoers? What is generally supposed is that Allah will judge between the believers on one hand and the unbelievers and wrongdoers on the other, because judgement will be given between them. But these words are about people who all deserve to be punished, so how will Allah judge between them? Look at the justice of Allah Almighty. Do not suppose that one who rejects Allah will not be punished when he wrongs an unbeliever like himself. Suppose that one unbeliever wrongs another unbeliever – will Allah Almighty leave this case and not take retaliation from the wrong-doer? We say "No," because Allah Almighty created all of us and lordship demands that He punish every wrongdoer and exact what is due to everyone who has been wronged, even if they reject Him.

Allah ﷻ says *"decided between them"*, and that means that there is something which demanded judgement. Judgement involves lack of bias and deciding between two litigants. Judgement entails a ruling. Because Allah ﷻ is the Lord of all and the Creator of all, everyone shares equally in the gift of His lordship. The sun shines on both believers and unbelievers. The rain falls on both believers and unbelievers. The air is breathed by both believers and unbelievers; because this is the gift of lordship. All people are the same in respect of it.

When a man wrongs another man, whether wrongdoer or wronged are believers or unbelievers, then Allah ﷻ must settle this injustice by His justice. Our Lord does not wrong anyone. He is the One who has commanded us to take on His qualities, one of which is justice. The Almighty says in His Eternal Book, *"Do not let hatred for a people incite you into not being just. Be just. That is closer to fear of Allah."* (5:8)[1]

1. Do not allow hatred for people to move you to be unjust so that you transgress against them. Whoever has a right must take it. When justice is sought from the opponent, it rebukes that opponent because he acts contrary to faith. It is certain that the litigant will say to himself: "The justice of this Muslim will not keep him from telling the truth. So his creed must make him a strong man and his *deen* which commands him to do that must be the best *deen*."

The repayment of those who are profligate in injustice

Allah Almighty says, *"That is how We repay anyone who is profligate and does not believe in the Signs of his Lord. And the punishment of the Next World is much harsher and longer lasting."* (20:127) That means, "We will repay the one who is profligate with the like of this repayment. Profligacy here means to exceed the limits in respect of a command which is known to have a logical limit. We eat in order to prolong our lives. When someone eats more than is necessary to ensure that aim, he becomes profligate. So profligacy is to exceed the desired limit in doing something. Take, for instance, a man's income. If he spends all of it and does not save any of it, he cannot improve his life or make his standard of living better. He cannot buy a car with which to move or build a house for himself and his children because he has spent all he earned and not kept anything in reserve.

But Islam teaches us balance in spending so that we spend a part of our income and keep part of it back. In respect of his spending, Allah Almighty wants a man to do two things: spend and not be extravagant, because if he does not spend, welfare in this world will cease, manufacture will stop, workers will be idle, and the means of acquiring provision will fail. When every man spends and buys what he needs, then the wheel of life revolves and continues. But he should not spend all that he gets. He should save something for times of need so that he can improve his life. Improvement is according to his livelihood. Then he will have enough for himself and his family to enjoy an honourable life.

Allah Almighty says, *"Those who, when they spend, are neither extravagant nor mean, but take a stance midway between the two"* (25:67) because if people are stingy, the movement of life stops. If they are profligate, they will live in regret and toil and will be unable to improve their lives. That is why Allah Almighty says, *"Do not keep your hand chained to your neck, but do not extend it to its full extent so that you sit there blamed and destitute."* (17:29)

When Allah ﷻ created man, He also created for him the basic elements of his life with respect to food, drink and air, and He appointed for him lawful food to eat and unlawful to keep his distance from. Part of the greatest profligacy is to turn to what Allah has made unlawful from what Allah has made lawful. One who does that exceeds the limit. You should not constrict yourselves by making unlawful for yourselves what Allah has made lawful, and not be profligate to yourselves by exceeding the limits and making lawful what Allah has made unlawful. All of that is in the best interest of this world and the Next for you.

When Allah ﷻ created man, He brought into existence the basic elements of his life, as He guaranteed for him that his species would remain as the human species and endure until the Final Hour. So He prescribed for him marriage by which he gains both pleasure and offspring, and appointed for him laws and limits respecting this area of life. So do not be profligate in this area and do not transgress in respect of the things which Allah has prohibited. One who is profligate in his life is someone who removes something from the domain of the forbidden to the area of the lawful, or moves something from the lawful to the domain of the forbidden.

Out of His mercy and kindness to His slave, Allah ﷻ tells him not to despair when he is profligate to himself and follows his appetites, and Shaytan makes attractive to him actions which are in opposition to what Allah has prescribed. So Allah ﷻ says, *"Say: 'O My slaves who have transgressed against yourselves, do not despair of the mercy of Allah. Truly Allah forgives all wrong actions.'"* (39:53) Allah ﷻ loves people when they repent and return to Him, for He accepts their repentance as long as they believe in Him and His Messenger ﷺ, whatever acts of disobedience they commit, provided they do not involve associating another with Him. Everyone who is profligate to himself, everyone who exceeds the *Shari'a* of his Lord, and everyone who transgresses against one of the rights of Allah Almighty or the rights of His creation should repent to Allah ﷻ and return to Him: perhaps Allah will turn to them and forgive them what they have done.

Allah says, *"That is how We repay anyone who is profligate and does not believe in the Signs of his Lord. And the punishment of the Next World is much harsher and longer lasting."* (20:127) He indicates that profligacy comes in the second rank after lack of faith, because by profligacy you move the unlawful to the lawful and the lawful to the unlawful. The meaning of that is that you disregard the *ayats* containing decrees.

Profligacy entails dissipation of the basic elements of life

The Almighty says, *"Our Lord, forgive us our wrong actions and any excesses we have gone to in what we have done."* (3:147) What is meant by excess in this context? It is any disobedience which is in excess of the basic elements of human life. Allah prescribed marriage for us for the sake of family and procreation to make existence flourish and enjoyment by obtaining what Allah Almighty has made lawful for us according to certain preconditions and defined rules. But when we take more than the prescribed number of wives, for instance, or take lovers rather than legal spouses, or we make matters difficult for those who want to marry, or we prefer something other than the guidance of Divine Law, that is excess in this regard.

Allah gave us the property which He allotted us. If we covet the property of someone else and take it from him without any right, this is something which causes enmity and hatred between people and cuts off ties of nearness and kinship, and it is transgression and profligacy. Allah has defined for us how to spend property, as He has defined income. If someone exceeds what Allah has defined and prescribed in the turnover of his property – if, for instance, he is one of those who deal with usury – that is one of the greatest transgressions regarding property. Profligacy occurs when someone takes something that he has no right to. That which is not your right and which Allah has not allotted you is not part of the requirements of your life and you can live without it.

Profligacy entails making corrupt choices

Those who are profligate against themselves regarding acts of disobedience do not summon before their mind's eyes the inevitable repayment for disobedience. That is why all the crimes committed by someone heedless of their consequences must be repaid. A criminal commits his crime and he supposes that he will be safe. A thief goes to steal thinking he is safe, but if he really felt that he was going to be arrested for it he would be most unlikely to do it. Allah ﷻ says, "Beware, O you who desire to distort the freedom of choice you have been given into diverting you from My Path by supposing that there will be no repayment for opposition to Me." Take this as a clear case and ask yourself how much benefit disobedience gives you and how much misery it gives you. Put the two together in the scales of the balance and you will know that the one which gives you the better and more lasting result is the one you must do. You must be far from what does not give you lasting good.

"Allah – there is no god but Him. He will gather you to the Day of Rising" (4:87) The Day of Rising is the Day about which Allah says, *"the Day mankind will stand before the Lord of all the worlds."* (83:6) The Day of Rising is the Day of Repayment on which Allah Almighty will repay those who did good and punish the those who did evil.

We will make a metaphor of this, not as an exact likeness, but as an approximation of what happens. A father gives his son a pound and tells him, "Buy what you want, but bear in mind that if you buy something useful, I will reward you for it. If you spend it on something corrupting, like playing cards or other such things, I will punish you." If the son immediately buys playing cards, is this a usurpation of his father's property? No, because the father gave him the choice. However, the son has done something which his father does not like. What then do you think about a slave of Allah when he follows the path of guidance which Allah Almighty has commanded him to follow? When the slave proceeds on the road of Straight Path, he does what Allah loves. When he leaves the Path by disobedience, he does what Allah does not love. If Allah had willed that all people follow guidance, He would have made them like angels.

Then one of the slaves is so bold as to cease to obey Allah. When a rebel commits an act of disobedience, he is able to do it because Allah Almighty created choice for him. So when someone says, "Every action is from Allah," this is a true statement. When the asker then asks, "So why then will we be punished?" the answer is that man did not direct his faculty of choice to what is good for him, but he instead chose to oppose the command of Allah. A knife, for instance, exists for slaughtering. If we slaughter a chicken with it, that does not merit punishment. If, however, we slaughter a human being with it, then we fall into the forbidden. Do we say to someone who brings a knife to the house, "You have brought an instrument of crime?" No: he brought a tool which can be used to do something useful or can be used as a means to commit a crime.

Consequently those who says that every action is from Allah speak the truth since the one who chooses can only act by his choice, because Allah Almighty gave His creation a choice. But does Allah ﷻ oblige him to commit the disobedience? No. Allah Almighty has set out the way for the right guidance of every man to the correct Path. When a man chooses something in opposition to the Path, it is his choice, and he is answerable and will be held to account for it.

Profligacy entails a man wronging himself

In the case of a man who is profligate to himself in taking forbidden things like wine, for instance, a time will come on him when he will have to deny himself things which are actually lawful to him. The doctor tells him, "You have destroyed your liver by drinking wine," and so it becomes forbidden to him to eat many lawful types of food and drink.

Therefore, this profligacy in reality entails a man wronging himself and results eventually in him being denied things which are lawful to him. Such a man has fallen into what Allah forbade and so Allah punishes him by denying him things which are lawful to him. So how much more will that be the case with respect to the punishment of the Next World?

Another example is the man who is profligate to himself by consuming a specific sort of food like sugar, for instance, eating far more than he needs to and eventually harming his health. The basic substance is a blessing from Allah Almighty to him but he did not take advantage of it by using it in balance. So the doctor may tell him, "You have taken more than your due. That is why your body has lost the power to use sugar properly and you have become ill. Avoid eating sweet things any more." A diabetic may continue to desire sweets and have the power to buy them, but they are forbidden to him. It is as if Allah Almighty is telling him, "By your wronging yourself, you have forbidden yourself what I made lawful to you."

So prohibition may occur through legislation, with the punishment for transgressing it decreed by the Lawgiver, or it may occur through the violation of natural limits, with the harmful effects following on automatically as a result. The latter occurs when profligacy in the matter comes from the self. We are always reciting this ayat: *"Because of wrongdoing on the part of the Jews, We made unlawful for them some good things which had previously been lawful for them."* (4:160)

The same applies to someone who takes property by means of usury. He takes property by usury in order to increase his own property. Here we ask him, "Why do you want wealth? Do you want it for the wealth itself or for another goal?" The sound view is that wealth is provision but not direct provision. Wealth is indirect provision because it buys things which we can use and consume which constitute direct provision. Imagine, for instance, that a man is in the desert and he has a mountain of gold with him but no food. In such a case the gold will be of no use. A loaf of bread and cup of water in such circumstances are far more valuable than gold. So wealth is provision but indirect provision, by means of which direct provision is obtained. Anyone who increases his wealth by usury must know that Allah ﷻ will obliterate it and that that wealth will be dissipated in calamities. Allah speaks the truth when He says, *"Allah obliterates usury but makes* sadaqa *grow in value!"* (2:276)

Man is the one who manages himself. If a man wants always to have what Allah has made lawful until the end of his life, he must not allow himself anything which Allah has forbidden him. By acting like that he will continue to enjoy the blessings of Allah upon him, for Allah Almighty says, *"Your Lord does not wrong His slaves."* (41:46) Man is the one who wrongs himself in accordance with the words of the Almighty, *"Allah does not wrong people in any way; rather it is people who wrong themselves."* (10:44)

Commentary on the *Hadith*:

"O My slaves! I have forbidden Myself injustice and I have made it unlawful between you..."

Shaykh Ibn Taymiyya

The Messenger of Allah ﷺ in what He related from His Almighty Lord said:

"O My slaves! I have forbidden Myself injustice and I have made it unlawful between you, so do not wrong one another. O My slaves! All of you are misguided except those that I guide, so seek My guidance and I will guide you. O My slaves! All of you are hungry except those that I feed, so ask me for food and I will feed you. O My slaves! All of you are naked except those that I clothe, so ask me for clothing and I will clothe you. O My slaves! You make mistakes by night and by day and I forgive all wrong actions, so ask for My forgiveness and I will forgive you. O My slaves! You will never attain to My harm so as to be able to harm Me, and you will never attain to My benefit so as to be able to benefit Me. O My slaves! If the first and last of you, all the *jinn* and all the men among you, possessed the heart of the most godfearing man among you, that would not increase My kingdom in any way. O My slaves! If the first and last of you, all the jinn and all the men among you, possessed the heart of the most evil man among you, that would not decrease My kingdom in any way. O My slaves! If the first and last of you, all the *jinn* and all the men among you, were to stand in a single place and ask of Me, I could give to every man what he asks without that decreasing what I have any more than a needle displaces when it enters the sea. O My slaves! It is your actions for which I call you to account and then repay you in full. So anyone who finds good should praise Allah, and anyone who finds something else should blame no one but himself."

Shaykh al-Islam Ibn Taymiyya said:

The words of the Almighty "O My slaves! I have forbidden Myself injustice" contain two great questions, each of which has subcategories and branches. One is about the injustice which Allah has forbidden Himself. He denies it to Himself when He says, *"We did not wrong them"* (16:118) and *"Your Lord will not wrong anyone at all"* (18:49). He says, *"Your Lord does not wrong His slaves."* (41:46) Allah says, *"Allah does not wrong anyone by so much as the smallest mote. And if there is a good deed Allah will multiply it…"* (4:40) Allah ﷻ states clearly that He does not desire it: *"Allah does not desire wrong for any being"* (3:108) and He says, *"Allah does not want any injustice for His slaves."* (40:31) He stills His slaves' fear of it by saying, *"But anyone who does right actions, being a believer, need fear no wrong or belittlement."* (20:112)

People disagree about the meaning of injustice in this context. The dispute is between two sides which are far apart but there is a middle ground between them, and "the best of matters are the middle ones." It is a matter of exploring fate (*qadar*) and marrying it to the *Shari'a*, since delving into that subject without full knowledge brings about misguidance for most ordinary people. That is why the Prophet ﷺ forbade his Companions to argue about it.

In the famous *hadith* concerning grief, the Messenger of Allah ﷺ said, "If care or sorrow afflicts a slave and he says, 'O Allah, I am Your slave, the son of your slave, the son of Your female slave. My forelock is in Your hand. Your judgement is carried out on me and Your decision for me is just. I ask You by every Name which is Yours, or which You revealed in Your Book or which You have taught to any of Your creation, or which You have kept to Yourself in the knowledge of the Unseen, that You make the Qur'an the life of my heart, the light of my breast, the removal of my sorrow and the departure of my care and sorrow,' Allah will remove his care and sorrow and replace it with happiness."[1] The Companions said, "Messenger of Allah, should we learn it?" He said, "Yes. Anyone who hears it should learn it."

He made it clear that every decision on the part of Allah about His slaves is just. This is why it is said, "Every blessing from Him is a favour. Every vengeance from Him is justice." It is also said, "I obey You by Your favour and grace, I disobey You by Your knowledge – or Your justice – and the proof is Yours. I ask You by the obligation of Your proof against me and the cutting off of my proof unless You forgive me."

This *hadith* contains many vital rules of the *deen* in respect of knowledge and actions, regarding both fundamentals and branches. That first sentence, which is "I have forbidden Myself injustice," encompasses most of the salient points about the Divine Attributes and *qadar*.

The second sentence, "I have made it unlawful between you, so do not wrong one another" encompasses all the *deen*. What Allah has forbidden is all injustice, and what He commands is all justice. The Almighty says, "*We sent Our Messengers with the Clear Signs and sent down the Book and the Balance with them so that mankind might establish justice. And We sent down iron, in which lie great force and many uses for mankind, so that Allah might know those who help Him and His Messengers in the Unseen.*" (57:25)

So Allah reported that He sent Messengers and sent down the Book and the Balance for people to establish justice. He mentioned that He sent down iron by which this truth is supported. The Book guides and the sword supports. Allah is enough of a guide and a helper. This is why people are sustained by the people of the Book and the people of iron, as was reported from the

1. Related by Ahmad in the *Musnad*, 1/391-452, from Ibn Mas'ud ﷺ. Shaykh Ahmad Shakir says that its *isnad* is sound.

Salaf: "If two groups are in order, then the whole people will be in order: the amirs and the scholars."[1]

Justice must be preceded by knowledge since someone without knowledge will not know what justice is. Man is unjust and ignorant except for the one to whom Allah turns and who thereby becomes a just person of knowledge. Such people become judges. Others fall into three categories: just scholars, the ignorant, and wrongdoers. The last two categories are among the people of the Fire, as the Prophet ﷺ said. What is assumed is that justice is reached by a man's exercising judgement. The Prophet ﷺ said, "When a judge exercises judgement and is right, he has two rewards. When he judges and exercises judgement and is wrong, he has one reward."[1]

Allah said, "O My slaves! All of you are hungry except those I feed, so ask me for food and I will feed you. O My slaves! All of you are naked except those that I clothe, so ask me for clothing and I will clothe you." This gives us two great principles. One is the obligation to rely on Allah for the kind of provision which is guaranteed to bring benefit, such as food, and also for the kind of provision which repels harm, such as clothing. The reason for this need to rely on Allah is that He does not determine an fixed amount of food and drink for each person. The amount obtained by particular people is due to particular causes which bring that about. This is why He says, *"It is the duty of the fathers to feed and clothe them with correctness and courtesy"* (2:233) and He says, *"Do not hand over to the simple-minded any property of theirs for which Allah has made you responsible, but provide for them and clothe them out of it."* (4:5) What is commanded is decreed for slaves. That is like what He says, *"And when they are told, 'Spend from the provision Allah has given you,' those who reject say to those who believe, 'Why should we feed someone whom, if He willed, Allah would*

1. It is related *marfu'* from the Prophet ﷺ and Abu Nu'aym transmitted it in *Hilyatu'l-awliya'*, 4/96 and Ibn 'Abdi'l-Barr in *Jami' bayan al-'ilm*, 1/184. Shaykh al-Albani related it in *hadiths* of weak and fabricated chains as number 16, and said that it is fabricated.

1. Al-Bukhari (7352, *Fath*) and Muslim (15/1716) transmitted it from 'Amr ibn al-'As.

Himself feed?'" (36:47) He blames those who disregard what is commanded, which would be a sufficient amount.

From this it is known that benefiting through a commanded cause or permitted cause is not incompatible with the obligation to rely on Allah. Our intrinsic poverty and need for Allah are affirmed along with the action of the cause, since there is nothing found in creatures which is by itself the complete reason for obtaining the goal. This is why it is not correct to connect events to their apparent causes without aknowledging their dependence on the will of Allah Almighty. What Allah wills comes about and what He does not will does not. Whoever thinks that he needs only the means and that reliance on Allah is not necessary has abandoned the reliance which Allah has made obligatory for him and has abandoned his obligation of *tawhid.* That is why such people are disappointed when they rely on causes. If anyone hopes for help or provision from a source other than Allah, Allah disappoints him. As 'Ali ﷺ said, "A slave should only place his hopes in his Lord and only fear his own wrong actions."

Allah ﷻ says: *"Say: 'So what do you really think? If Allah desires harm for me, can those you call upon besides Allah remove His harm? Or if He desires mercy for me, can they withhold His mercy?' Say: 'Allah is enough for me. All who truly trust put their trust in Him.'"* (39:37) This is also true of anyone who takes up reliance but abandons the means which we are commanded to take. He is also an ignorant wrongdoer who disobeys Allah by failing to do what He has commanded. The action which is commanded is worship of Allah. Allah says, *"So worship Him and put your trust in Him."* (11:123) Does someone who does something he has been commanded to do while abandoning reliance incur a worse sin than someone who does what he is commanded, relying on Allah, and leaving the means he has been commanded to use? Both of them neglect part of what is mandatory for them: they share in a kind of wrong action. So that one may be more blameworthy or it may be the other. Reliance is in reality a sort of means.

Abu Dawud related in his *Sunan* that the Prophet ﷺ decided between two men and that the one against whom judgement was given said when he turned away, "Allah is enough for me, and how excellent a guardian!" The Prophet ﷺ said, "Allah censures powerlessness. You must be astute. If someone overpowers you, then say, 'Allah is enough for me and the best guardian.'"[1]

In *Sahih Muslim* Abu Hurayra ﷺ reported that the Prophet ﷺ said, "A strong believer is better and more beloved to Allah than a weak believer although there is good in both. Desire what will bring you benefit and seek help from Allah and do not give way to helplessness. If something happens to you, do not say 'If only I had done such-and-such.' Say instead, 'The decree of Allah; He does as He wills.' Otherwise you will expose yourself to the action of Shaytan."[2]

The words of the Prophet ﷺ, "Desire what will bring you benefit and seek help from Allah and do not give way to helplessness", is a command to use the means that we are required to that. It is to be eager for benefits. Along with that, one is commanded to rely on Him, and that is seeking the help of Allah. Whoever is content to comply with only one of them has disobeyed one of the two commands. He forbade helplessness which is the opposite of astuteness, as He said in the other *hadith*, "Allah censures powerlessness. You must be astute." As we find what is called in the Syrian *hadith*, "The astute person is the one who gains control over himself and works for what is after death. The incapable person is the one who follows the desires of his self and wishfully puts his hope in Allah."[3]

The incapable person in the *hadith* is the opposite of the astute person. Anyone who says that what is meant by incapable here is the opposite of pious has twisted the *hadith* and not prop-

1. Abu Dawud related this *hadith* (3627) from 'Awf ibn Malik. Al-Albani holds that it is weak.

2. Muslim 34/2664.

3. Ibn Majah (4660) from Shaddad ibn Aws. Al-Albani holds that it is weak.

erly understood it. Connected to this is the *hadith*, "Everything is by a decree – even helplessness and astuteness."[1]

Also connected to it is the report which al-Bukhari related in his *Sahih* from Ibn 'Abbas, may Allah be pleased with both hm and his father: "The people of Yemen used to go on *hajj* and not take provision. They would say, 'We are relying on Allah.' When they came to Makka, they begged from people."[2]

Allah ﷻ says about this, "*Take provision, but the best provision is fear of Allah.*" (2:197). Whoever does as he is commanded with respect to taking provision and then uses it to seek help in obeying Allah and gives charity from it to those in need, obeys Allah in two ways, unlike the one who abandons taking provision in favour of turning to the provision of other people performing *hajj*, thus in fact relying on other people. If the heart of that person does not turn to a particular helper, he turns to them as a whole. But if someone takes provision without the mandatory reliance on Allah and without assisting the needy, then he is in the same category as someone who has neglected the commanded provision, because he too has failed to do something he was commanded to do.

Apart from them, we also find people who consider supplication to be a shortcoming and breach in the case of the elite, thinking the state of the elite is to take what is decreed for them (without asking for anything more) when it says in this *hadith*, "All of you are hungry except those that I feed so ask me for food and I will feed you," and "Ask me for clothing and I will clothe you." Accordingtp at-Tabarani and others, the Prophet ﷺ said, "Each one of you should ask his Lord for all his needs, even the strap of his sandal if it is cut. If He does not make it easy, it will not be made easy."[3]

1. Part of a *hadith* transmitted by Muslim (18/2655) from 'Abdullah ibn 'Amr.

2. Al-Bukhari 1451.

3. Ibn Hibban related it in his *Sahih* (866) from Anas, as did Abu Ya'la in his *Musnad* (3403). Shaykh Husayn Asad said that its *isnad* is sound according to the preconditions of Muslim.

Everyone is obliged to seek the guidance of Allah and act to obey Him in it. The view of those people would entail the rejection of something which is a general command. Indeed their view is a rejection of what is both created and commanded. They have erred by supposing that the prior decree of destiny precludes the existence of a cause which is commanded. That is like someone who is a *zindiq* and abandons obligatory actions, on the grounds that the divine decree has already decided who the blessed and the damned are. He does not understand that the decree preceded the things on which it is based.

At-Tirmidhi related from Abu Khuzayma from his father who said, "I asked the Prophet ﷺ, "Messenger of Allah, what do you think about these remedies with which we treat ourselves and the talismans which we make, or any act of piety we perform? Will they avert any of the decree of Allah?" He answered, "They are part of what Allah has decreed."[1]

He said, "O My slaves, you err by night and day and I forgive all wrong actions." One variant has, "I forgive wrong actions, and I do not care. So ask My forgiveness and I will forgive you."

General forgiveness of all sins is of two types. One type is forgiveness for one who repents, as the Almighty says, *"Say: 'O My slaves who have transgressed against yourselves, do not despair of the mercy of Allah. Truly Allah forgives all wrong actions. He is the Ever-Forgiving, the Most Merciful.' Turn to your Lord and submit to Him before the punishment comes upon you, for then you cannot be helped."* (39:53-54) Its context, along with the reason for the revelation of the *ayat*, makes the meaning clear: a wrongdoer should not despair of the forgiveness of Allah, even if his wrong actions are numerous. Allah ﷻ does not consider any wrong action too terrible to forgive his repentant slave for. Included in this generality are *shirk* and all other wrong actions. Allah Almighty forgives whoever repents of it for that as well.

In the second type of general forgiveness which is indicated by His words, "O My slaves, you err by night and day and I

1. At-Tirmidhi (2148) and Ibn Majah (3437). The variant is his. Al-Albani says that it is weak.

forgive all wrong actions," forgiveness means to lighten the punishment or to defer it to a stated term. This is absolutely general. That is why the Prophet ﷺ interceded for Abu Talib when he died as an idolater, and he was moved from the throes of the Fire until he was in the shallowest part of the Fire, wearing on his feet two sandals of fire which make his brains boil. He said, "If it had not been for me, he would have been in the lowest depth of the Fire."[1]

This meaning is indicated by the words of the Almighty, *"If Allah were to take mankind to task for what they have earned, He would not leave a single creature upon it."* (35:45) *"If Allah were to punish people for their wrong actions, not a single creature would be left on earth."* (16:61) And *"Any disaster that strikes you is through what your own hands have earned; and He pardons much."* (42:30)

Allah has said, "O My slaves! You will never attain to My harm so as to be able to harm Me and you will never attain to My benefit so as to be able benefit Me." By that Allah makes it clear that in the case of those to whom He is good by answering supplication and forgiving errors, He seeks no recompense from them for bringing benefit or repelling harm, which is the custom of a creature who gives benefit to another so that he will give him a benefit in repayment, or removes a harm from him so as to be protected from his harm. Allah has said, "You will never attain to My harm so as to be able to harm Me and you will never attain to My benefit so as to be able benefit Me."

Qatada said, "Allah does not command His slaves to do what He has commanded them to do because of any need He has of them, nor does He forbid them what He has forbidden them to do out of miserliness towards them; but He has commanded them to do things which entail their welfare and has forbidden them what would corrupt them."

1. Muslim (213/364) from an-Nu'man ibn Bashir. He related that the Messenger of Allah ﷺ said, "The person in the Fire with the least punishment will have two sandals with straps of fire by which his brains will boil, as a kettle boils. He does not think that anyone has a worse punishment than him, and yet he is the least of them in respect of punishment." He clearly stated the name of Abu Talib in the *hadith* of al-Hakim (4:625/8735) and in al-*Muntakhab* from the *Musnad* of 'Abd ibn Humayd. (711)

Allah has said, "O My slaves! If the first and last of you, all the *jinn* and all the men among you, possessed the heart of the most godfearing man among you, that would not increase My kingdom in any way. O My slaves! If the first and last of you, all the jinn and all the men among you, possessed the heart of the most evil man among you, that would not decrease My kingship in any way." "Kingship" here signifies the power to act and manage, and by it is meant managing and disposition itself. What is also meant by it is that which is subjected to the power, meaning the place where the management occurs. The statement covers all these things.

In any case, the piety of the pious and the impiety of the impious do not cause either increase or decrease in anything. It is Allah's will and power which bring things about. He creates whatever He wishes. If Allah had wished to prevent the impiety of the impious, nothing could stop that, as kings can forbid injustice for their subjects which is contrary to what they themselves would choose for themselves. If He had so wished, He could have created none of the things He did create on account of the piety of the pious. He has no need of their piety to do that. He needs no helper as kings need and seek the help of a large number of obedient subjects.

He said, "If the first and last of you, all the jinn and all the men among you, possessed the heart of the most evil man among you, that would not decrease My kingdom in any way. O My slaves! If the first and last of you, all the *jinn* and all the men among you, were to stand in a single place and ask of Me, I could give to every man what he asks without that decreasing what I have by any more than a needle displaces when it enters the sea."

Allah makes it clear that if all creatures were to ask when they are in the same place at the same time and He were to give every one of them what he asked for, that would not decrease what He has except as when a needle is dipped into the sea. There are two views about His words, "without that decreasing what I have". One is that it indicates that what He has are things which exist and which He gives to them when they ask. According to this, the word "decrease" is as its normal meaning is because the giving in this case is from having a lot. If had been only a little, then it would have been something which would have been decreased. If someone relates, "without that decreasing My kingdom," it is applied to what He has, as in this expression. His words "what I have" are particular, which is not the case with His words, "My kingdom".

Then He concludes by confirming what He has explained about His justice and beneficence. He said, "O My slaves! It is your actions for which I call you to account and then repay you in full. So anyone who finds good should praise Allah, and anyone who finds something else should blame none but himself." Allah makes it clear that He is good to His slaves in repaying them for their righteous actions with a beneficence by which He deserves praise. For He is the Blesser by commanding them and guiding His slaves to them and helping them to achieve them, and then He counts them and pays them in full.

All of that is bounty and beneficence on His part, since every blessing from Him is excellence and every act of revenge from Him is justice. Even though "He has prescribed mercy for Himself," and "it is His obligation to help the believers," as was already made clear, that is not obligatory like the obligation of the rights people owe to one another which is justice and not bounty. His beneficence is the best and He is beneficent by making it a duty for Himself and prescribing it for Himself. He has prescribed mercy for Himself and made it a duty for Himself to help His believing slaves. One like that is beneficent with a beneficence topped by yet more beneficence.

Just as it is clear that He is beneficent by commanding good actions and His beneficence is completed by His counting them and then rewarding them, so it is also clear that He is just in repaying evil deeds. He has said, "Anyone who finds something else should blame no one but himself." It is as He has explained in the like of His words, *"We did not wrong them, but they wronged themselves."* (11:101) It is on this principle that the Shari'a is based, which is harmony with the natural form of Allah in which He formed His creation.[1]

1. *The Collection of the Fatwas of Shaykh al-Islam Ibn Taymiyya*, 18/136:20.

Ibn Rajab says:

Imam Ahmad said, "This is the most noble *hadith* of the people of Syria." The Prophet ﷺ said in what he related from his Lord: "O My slaves! I have forbidden injustice to Myself," meaning that He has forbidden Himself to be unfair to His slaves: as He says, *"I do not wrong My slaves."* (50:29) He also says, *"Allah does not desire wrong for any being"* (3:108); and *"Allah does not want any injustice for His slaves."* (40:31) He says, *"Your Lord does not wrong His slaves,"* (41:46) and *"Allah does not wrong anyone by so much as the smallest mote."* (4:40) He also says, *"But anyone who does right actions, being a believer, need fear no wrong or any belittlement."* (20:112) "Belittlement" here refers to being shortchanged in respect of the repayment for good deeds. "Wrong" here means being punished for the wrong actions of someone else.

This kind of statement is frequent in the Qur'an. It suggests that Allah potentially has the power to be unjust but does not exercise it – as a favour from Himself and generosity, nobility and beneficence to His slaves.

Many scholars explain injustice as being to put things in what is not their proper place. As for those who explain it as meaning disposing of the property of another without his permission – and the like of that is transmitted from Iyas ibn Mu'awiya and others – they say that injustice is impossible for Him and conceivable for others, since all that He does entails His disposal of His kingdom which is entirely His property.

He says, "I have made it unlawful between you, so do not wrong one another," which means that Allah Almighty made injustice unlawful to His slaves and forbade them to wrong one another in their mutual dealings. Thus it is unlawful for anyone to wrong another, while wronging oneself is also absolutely forbidden. Injustice is of two types. One is the injustice towards one's self. The greatest form of that is *shirk*, as the Almighty says, *"Attri-buting partners to Him is a terrible wrong."* (31:13) The *mushrik* places a creature in the place of the Creator and worships it, taking it as a God. He puts things in what is not their proper place. Most of of the threats to the wrongdoers mentioned in the Qur'an refer to the idolaters. As Allah Almighty says, *"It is the unbelievers who are the wrongdoers."* (2:254) That is followed by the different sorts of acts of disobedience, major and minor.

The second type of injustice is the injustice of one person to another as mentioned in this *hadith*. The Prophet ﷺ said in his *khutba* in the Farewell *Hajj*, "Allah has made your blood, property and honour sacred like the sacredness of this day in this month in this land of yours." It is related that he said that on the Day of Sacrifice or the Day of 'Arafa or on the second day of the days of *Tashriq*. In one transmission we find: "Then he said, 'Listen to Me. Live. Do not wrong one another. The property of a Muslim is not lawful except when he is cheerful about it."

In the *Sahih* collections, Ibn 'Umar رضي الله عنه reported that the Prophet ﷺ said, "Injustice will be darkness on the Day of Rising." In both of them, Abu Musa رضي الله عنه reported that the Prophet ﷺ said, "Allah prolongs the life of the unjust but when He takes them, He will not let them escape." Then he recited, *"Such is the seizing of your Lord when He seizes the cities which do wrong. His seizing is painful, violent."* (11:102) In the *Sahih* collection of al-Bukhari, Abu Dharr رضي الله عنه related that the Prophet ﷺ said, "Whoever has done an injustice to his brother should seek to be absolved by him before the day when there will be neither dinar nor dirham, and when some of his good deeds will be taken for his brother. If he does not have any good actions, some of the bad actions of his brother will be taken and cast onto him."

Allah ﷻ said, "O My slaves! I have forbidden injustice to Myself and I have made it unlawful between you, so do not wrong one another. O My slaves! All of you are misguided except those that I guide, so seek My guidance and I will guide you. O My slaves! All of you are hungry except those that I feed, so ask me for food and I will feed you. O My slaves! All of you are naked except those that I clothe, so ask me for clothing and I will clothe you. O My slaves! You make mistakes by night and by day and I forgive all wrong actions, so ask for My forgiveness and I will forgive you."

This makes it clear that all creation is in need of Allah Almighty to provide them with what benefits them and repel what harms them in the matters of their *deen* and this world. His slaves control nothing of that for themselves. If Allah does not show favour to someone by giving him guidance and provision, he is deprived of them in this world and is one of those to whom Allah does not show mercy by forgiving his wrong actions or errors in the Next World.

Allah Almighty says, *"Anyone Allah guides, he is truly guided. But anyone He misguides, you will find no protector for him to give him right guidance."* (18:17) There are many such examples in the Qur'an. The Almighty says, *"Whatever mercy Allah opens up to people no one can withhold, and whatever He withholds no one can afterwards release. He is the Almighty, the All-Wise."* (25:2) He says, *"There is no creature on the earth that is not dependent upon Allah for its provision."* (11:6) Allah Almighty says, relating from Adam and his wife, peace be upon both of them that, *"They said, 'Our Lord, we have wronged ourselves. If you do not forgive us and have mercy on us, we will be among the lost.'"* (7:23) and that Nuh, peace be upon him, said, *"If You do not forgive me and have mercy on me, I will be among the lost."* (11:47)

Ibrahim the Khalil,[1] peace be upon him, provided evidence of the oneness of Allah and concluded that there is no god but Him and that every thing associated with Him is false. He said to his people: *"Have you really thought about what you worship, you and your fathers who came before? They are all my enemy – except for the Lord of all the worlds: He who created me and guides me; He who gives me food and gives me drink; and when I am ill, it is He who heals me; He who will cause my death, then give me life; He who I sincerely hope will forgive my mistakes on the Day of Reckoning. My Lord, give me right judgement and unite me with the righteous."* (26:75-82)

1. *"The close friend," a title of the Prophet Ibrahim, "the Friend of Allah".*

The One who alone created the human being, guided him, gave him life and will make him die in this world, and forgives his wrong actions in the Next World is alone entitled to divinity, worship, supplication and submission. Allah Almighty says: *"Allah is He who created you, then provides for you, then will cause you to die and then bring you back to life. Can any of your partner-gods do any of that? Glory be to Him and exalted is He above anything they associate with Him!"* (30:40)

The *hadith* contains evidence that Allah wants His slaves to ask Him for all their benefits in their *deen* and this world: food, drink, clothing and other things which they ask Him for as they ask Him for guidance and forgiveness. In another *hadith* we find: "Each of you should ask his Lord for all his needs, even his sandal strap when it is cut." Some *Salaf* used to ask Allah in their prayers for all their needs, even the salt for the dough of their bread and the fodder for their sheep.

He said, "All of you are misguided except those that I guide…" Some think that this conflicts with the *hadith* of 'Iyad ibn Himar from the Prophet ﷺ in which Allah says, "I created My slaves as *hanifs* (One variant has "Muslims"), and then Shaytans incited them." It is not like that. Allah created the sons of Adam and made them naturally disposed to accept Islam and incline to it rather than other things and they are predisposed to it and have the strength for it.

Each slave of Allah, however, must actually learn Islam. Before learning, he is ignorant. He does not know, as Allah Almighty says, *"Allah brought you out of your mothers' wombs knowing nothing at all."* (16:78) He said to His Prophet ﷺ, *"Did He not find you wandering and guide you?"* ((3:7). What is meant by this is that He found him not knowing what He later taught him of the Book and Wisdom. As the Almighty says, *"Accordingly We have revealed to you a Spirit by Our command. You had no idea of what the Book was, or faith. But We have made it a Light by which We guide those of Our slaves whom We will."* (42:52)

The human being is born naturally formed to accept the Truth. Allah's guiding Him may take the form of someone who teaches him guidance so that he becomes guided by action after he was guided by nature. If Allah does not desire guidance for him, He sends him someone who will impart to him something other than the natural form, as the Prophet ﷺ said: "Every child is born on the natural form and then his parents make him a Jew, a Christian or a Magian."

As for the believer asking Allah for guidance, there are two types of guidance. There is general guidance, which is guidance to Islam and faith which all believers share in; and there is specific guidance, which is guidance to knowledge of the details of the different areas of faith and Islam and being helped to do that. This is needed by every believer, night and day. This is why Allah commanded His slaves to recite in every *rak'at* of their prayer: *"Guide us on the Straight Path."* (1:6) The Prophet ﷺ said in his supplication at night, "Guide me to the truth about disagreements by Your permission. You guide whomever You wish to a Straight Path." This is why he blessed people when they sneezed and said to him, "May Allah guide you," as has come in the *Sunna*. The Prophet ﷺ instructed 'Ali to ask Allah for correctness and guidance and taught al-Hasan to say in the *qunut* of the *witr*, "O Allah, guide me among those You have guided."

As for asking forgiveness for wrong actions, it is to seek pardon. The slave of Allah is most in need of that because he errs by night and day. Repentance, asking forgiveness, and the command and encouragement to do them are repeatedly mentioned in the Qur'an. At-Tirmidhi and Ibn Majah related in a *hadith* from Anas ﷺ that the Prophet ﷺ said, "All of the sons of Adam err. The best of those who err are those who repent." Al-Bukhari transmitted from a *hadith* of Abu Hurayra ﷺ that the Prophet ﷺ said, "By Allah, I ask forgiveness of Allah and I turn to Him a hundred times every day."

He transmitted from a *hadith* of al-Agharr al-Muzani ﷺ that he heard the Prophet ﷺ say, "O people, turn to your Lord and ask His forgiveness. I turn to Allah and ask His forgiveness a hundred times a day." An-Nasa'i transmitted it as, "O people, turn to your Lord in repentance and ask His forgiveness a hundred times every day."

Imam Ahmad transmitted from a *hadith* of Hudhayfa ﷛ that he used to say, "I had a sharpness in my tongue towards my family which I did not direct to others. I mentioned that to the Prophet ﷺ, who said, 'Where are you in respect to asking for forgiveness, Hudhayfa? I ask forgiveness of Allah a hundred times a day.'" Abu Bakr ﷛ reported that the Prophet ﷺ said, "I ask forgiveness of Allah a hundred times and I turn to Him."

An-Nasa'i related that Abu Musa ﷛ said, "While we were sitting, the Prophet ﷺ came and said, 'There is no morning but that I ask forgiveness of Allah a hundred times." Imam Ahmad, Abu Dawud, at-Tirmidhi, an-Nasa'i and Ibn Majah related from the *hadith* of Ibn 'Umar ﷛ that he said, "We used to count the Messenger of Allah ﷺ saying in one gathering a hundred times, 'Lord, forgive me and turn to me. You are the Ever-Turning, the Most Merciful.'"

An-Nasa'i related from a *hadith* of Abu Hurayra ﷛ that he said about the Messenger of Allah ﷺ, "How often he would say, 'I ask forgiveness of Allah and I turn to him!'" Imam Ahmad related from a *hadith* of 'A'isha ﷛ that the Prophet ﷺ said, "O Allah, make me one of those who are given good news when they do good deeds and ask forgiveness when they do bad."

The *hadith* continues: "O My slaves! You will never attain to My harm so as to be able to harm Me and you will never attain to My benefit so as to be able benefit Me." Allah Almighty is Rich and Praiseworthy in Himself. He has no need of the obedience of His slaves and His benefit does not return to Him. Rather they benefit by it. He is not harmed by their disobedience but they are harmed by it.

Allah Almighty says, *"Do not let those who rush headlong into unbelief sadden you. They do not harm Allah in any way."* (3:176) He also says, *"Those who turn on their heels do not harm Allah in any way."* (3:144) The Prophet ﷺ used to say in his *khutba*, "Whoever disobeys Allah and His Messenger has erred and harmed only himself and does not harm Allah at all." Allah

Almighty says, *"But if you disbelieve, everything in the heavens and everything in the earth belongs to Allah. Allah is Rich beyond need, Praiseworthy."* (4:131) Allah says, relating from Musa, *"Musa said, 'If you were to be ungrateful, you and everyone on the earth, Allah is Rich beyond need, Praiseworthy.'"* (14:8) Allah Almighty says, *"But if anyone disbelieves, Allah is Rich beyond need of any being."* (3:97) *"Their flesh and blood does not reach Allah but your fear of Him does reach Him."* (22:37)

Allah obliges His slaves to fear Him and obey Him just as He dislikes them to disobey Him. That is why He is more happy about the repentance of those who repent than the joy of someone whose camel which carries his food and drink and has got lost in a desert and he has looked for it until he is unable to do more and has despaired of it. He has resigned himself to death and despaired of life, then sleep overcomes him and he falls asleep and wakes up to find his lost camel standing beside him. This is the greatest example of joy a creature can imagine.

All of this is connected with His lack of need of the acts of obedience of His slaves and the fact that He returns the benefit of doing them to them rather than Himself. This is part of His perfect generosity and beneficence to His slave and His love of helping them and repelling harm from them. He wants His slaves to recognise Him, love Him, fear Him, obey Him and draw near to Him. He wants them to know that only He forgives wrong actions and that only He has the power to forgive the wrong actions of His slaves, as in the variant of this *hadith* from 'Abdu'r-Rahman ibn Ghanim from Abu Dharr: "If any of you know that I have the power to forgive and then asks for My forgiveness, I will forgive him without caring."

In the *Sahih*, it is reported that the Prophet ﷺ said, "A slave commits a wrong action and says, 'O Lord, I have committed a wrong action, so forgive me!' Allah says, 'My slave knows that he has a Lord who forgives wrong actions and punishes wrong actions. I have forgiven My slave.'" In a *hadith* from 'Ali ibn Abi Talib رضي الله عنه he reported about the Prophet ﷺ, "When he got on his mount, he praised Allah three times and said the *takbir* three times. He said, 'Glory be to You! I have wronged myself, so forgive me. Only You forgive wrong actions.' Then he smiled. He said, 'Your Lord likes His slave to say, "Lord, forgive me my wrong actions," saying, 'He knows that only I forgive wrong actions.'" Imam Ahmad and at-Tirmidhi, who says it is sound, related in the *Sahih* from the Prophet ﷺ, "By Allah, Allah is more merciful to His slaves than a mother is to her child."

One of the companions of Dhu'n-Nun used to go around calling, "O where is my heart? Who will find my heart!" One day he went to one of the lanes of Cairo and found a child weeping while his mother was beating him. Then she threw him out of the house and locked the door. The child began to look right and left, not knowing where to go or what to aim for. He returned to the door of the house and began to weep, saying, "Mother! Who will open the door for me if you close your door to me. Who will bring me near if you are angry with me?" His mother had mercy and looked through the crack of the door and saw her child with tears running down his cheeks, dragging in the dust. So she opened the door, sat him on her lap and began to kiss him, saying, "My dear, precious, it was you who provoked me against yourself and you who disobeyed what is allowed for you. If you had obeyed me, I would not have done anything nasty to you." Then the young man was ecstatic and shouted, "I have found my heart! I have found my heart!"

Reflect on the words of the Almighty, *"Those who, when they act indecently or wrong themselves, remember Allah and ask forgiveness for their bad actions – and who can forgive bad actions except Allah? – and do not knowingly persist in what they were doing."* (3:135) This contains an indication that wrongdoers have no one to seek refuge with or rely on for forgiveness for their wrong actions other than Allah. That is also clear in what He says about the three who stayed behind (the expedition to Tabuk), *"And also towards the three who were left behind, so that when the earth became narrow for them, for all its great breadth, and their own selves became constricted for them and they realised that there was no refuge from Allah except in Him, He turned towards them so that they might turn to Him. Allah is the Ever-Relenting, the Most Merciful."* (9:118)

He connected His relenting towards them with their understanding that there is no refuge from Allah except in Him. When someone fears a creature, he flees from him to another. When someone fears Allah, there is no one with whom he can seek refuge. There is nowhere that he can flee to except from Him to Him. It is as the Prophet ﷺ said in his supplication, "There is no refuge and no escape from You except to You," and he said, "I seek refuge with Your pleasure from Your wrath, and with Your pardon from Your punishment, and with You from You."

Al-Fudayl ibn 'Iyad ﵁ said, "There is no night when the darkness deepens and night lowers its cover but that the Majestic – may His majesty be exalted! – calls out, "Who has greater generosity than Me? Even if creatures disobey Me, I still watch over them, and I feed them while they lie in their beds as if they had not disobeyed Me. I undertake to preserve them as if they had not sinned regarding what was between Me and them. I am generous with favour towards the rebel and I am gracious to the wrongdoer. Who is there who has called on Me whom I have not answered? Who is there who has asked of Me to whom I not given? Who is there who has knelt at my door whom I have then driven away? I am the Bountiful and bounty is from Me. I am the Generous and generosity is from Me. I am the Noble and nobility is from Me. Part of My nobility is that I forgive rebels after they have rebelled. Part of My generosity is that I give the slave what he asks for and I give him what he does not ask Me for. Part of My nobility is that I make the repentant as if he had not disobeyed Me. Where will creatures flee, other than to Me? At whose door will rebels seek refuge?" Abu Nu'aym transmitted it.

Someone else said, along those lines: "I did evil and did not do good, and have come to You in repentance. I am a slave who had run away from his master, now hoping for forgiveness. If his hope is disappointed, then there is no one on the earth who suffers greater disappointment."

The *hadith* continues after that, "O My slaves! If the first and last of you, all the *jinn* and all the men among you, possessed the heart of the most godfearing man among you, that would not increase My kingdom in any way. O My slaves! If the first and last of you, all the jinn and all the men among you, possessed the heart of the most evil man among you, that would not decrease My kingdom in any way."

This indicates that His kingdom would not be increased by the obedience of all creation, even if they were all godfearing and pious and had hearts like that of the most godfearing of them. Likewise, His kingdom would not be decreased by the disobedience of the disobedient, even if all jinn and men were corrupt rebels had hearts like that of the most impious of them. Allah is Rich beyond Need of other than Himself. He has absolute perfection in His Essence, Attributes and Actions. His kingdom is a complete kingdom with no need of increase or decrease in any aspect or in any way.

Some people say that His bringing His creation into existence in the way He has is more perfect than bringing it into existence in any other way. It is the best of all possible worlds. The evil it contains is relative evil: evil in relation to some things rather than others. It is not absolute evil so that its non-existence would have been better than its existence. Its existence is indeed better than its non-existence. This is the meaning of His words, "Good is in His hand."

The meaning of the words of the Prophet ﷺ, "Evil is not attributable to You," refers to pure evil whose non-existence is better than its existence. That does not exist in Allah's kingdom. Allah Almighty brought His creation into existence according to what His wisdom and justice demand. He singled out some people whom He created for His favour and left others of them to His justice by the far-reaching wisdom that it contained. This question is unresolved.

It differs from what is in the *hadith* stating that even if all creation were to have the quality of the most perfect of His creation in piety and *taqwa*, that would not increase His kingdom at all, not even by the amount of a gnat's wing. If they were to have the quality of the most imperfect of creation in corruption, that would not decrease His kingdom at all. It indicates that His kingdom is perfect in every single aspect, and does not increase and is not completed by obedience or decreased by acts of disobedience; and that nothing affects it.

These words contain an indication that the root of *taqwa* and impiety is found in the heart. When a heart is good and godfearing, the limbs are good. When the heart is impious, then the limbs are impious, as the Prophet ﷺ said, "*Taqwa* is here," pointing to his breast.

Allah ﷻ said, "If the first and last of you, all the *jinn* and all the men among you, were to stand in a single place and ask of Me, I could give to every man what he asks without that decreasing what I have by any more than a needle displaces when it enters the sea." What is meant by this is that He mentions the perfection of His power and the perfection of His kingdom; and that His kingdom and treasures do not run out and are not decreased by giving, even if He were to give to the first and the last of both jinn and men all of what they asked in one place at one time. That encourages people to ask Him and present their needs to Him.

In the two *Sahih* Collections, Abu Hurayra ؓ reported that the Prophet ﷺ said, "Allah's hand is not decreased by His spending night and day. Look at what He has spent since He created the heavens and the earth! It has not decreased what is in His hand."

In the *Sahih* Collection of Muslim, Abu Hurayra ؓ reported that the Prophet ﷺ said, "When anyone of you makes supplication, he should not say, 'O Allah, forgive me if You wish.' He should be firm and have great expectations. Allah does not consider anything too great." Abu Sa'id al-Khudri ؓ said, "When you call on Allah, increase your asking. What is in His keeping is not exhausted by anything. When you make supplication, be firm. Allah cannot be compelled."

In some of the Israelite material, Allah ﷻ says, "How can anyone place their hopes in other than Me regarding calamities, when calamities are in My Hand and I am the Living, the Self-Sustaining? How can anyone hope for good from another than Me and knock at his door in the morning, when in My hands are the keys to all treasures and My door is open to anyone who calls on Me? Why not put your hope in me regarding a disaster which is subject to my decision? Why not put your hope in me regarding something terrible which I decide? Who knocks on My door without My opening it to him? I am the repository of hopes, so how can hopes be cut off before reaching Me? Am I miserly, that My slave should find Me miserly? Are not this world, the Next World, generosity and favour all Mine? What prevents those who hope from placing their hope in Me? If the people of the heavens and the earth were to join together and I were to give each of them what I give all of them, and each had excessive desires, that would not decrease My kingdom by the extent of the leg of an ant. How can My kingdom be reduced when I sustain it? How great is the dejection of those who despair of My mercy! How great is the despair of those who disobey Me and leap towards things I have forbidden!"

His words, "without that decreasing what I have by any more than a needle displaces when it enters the sea", are to ascertain that what He has does not decrease in any way at all. As Allah says, *"What is with you comes to an end, but what is with Allah goes on for ever."* (16:96) When a needle is dipped into the sea and then brought out, that does not decrease the sea at all. In the same way, if a sparrow were to drink from it, for instance, that would not decrease the sea. This is why al-Khidr used this example with Musa, peace be upon him, when comparing their knowledge with the knowledge of Allah ﷻ. This is because the sea continues to be reinforced by the waters and rivers of this world. Whenever something is taken from it, it does not decrease it all because it is resupplied with more than what is taken from it. That is how it is with the food of the people of the Garden and what is in it. It is not decreased: as the Almighty says, *"fruits in abundance never failing, unrestricted."* (56:32-33)

A *hadith* states: 'Whenever you pluck a fruit, one like it returns to its place." It is related as: "Two like it and so it never decreases." That is attested to by the words of the Prophet ﷺ in the *khutba* of the eclipse: "I saw the Garden and reached for one of its bunches of fruit. If I had taken it, I would have eaten from it as long as this world lasts." This was transmitted in the two *Sahih* collections from the *hadith* of Ibn 'Abbas ﷺ. Imam Ahmad related it from a *hadith* of Jabir, which says, "If I had taken it, those between the heaven and the earth would have eaten from it without diminishing it at all." It is the same with the flesh of birds which the people of the Garden eat. They are replaced and revert to being alive, and none of them are decreased.

This *hadith* is related from the Prophet ﷺ theough chains of transmission in which there is some weakness, according to Ka'b. It is also related from Abu Umama al-Bahili from his people that Abu Umama said, "It is the same with whatever he drinks in it until his last breath. It then returns to being as it was." One of the righteous scholars was seen in a dream some time after his death. He said, "I have not eaten anything since the time I left you except for some chicken. As you know, the food of the Garden does not run out."

The reason why what is with Allah does not decrease by giving is clear in a *hadith qudsi* which at-Tirmidhi and Ibn Majah related in which Allah says, "That is because I am generous, existing and glorious. I do what I will. My gift is words and My punishment is words. My command to a thing when I will it is that I say to it, 'Be' and it is." This is like the words of the Almighty, *"His command when He desires a thing is simply to say to it, 'Be!' and it is."* (36:82) The Almighty else says, *"Our Word to a thing when We desire it is simply to say to it, 'Be!' and it is."* (16:40)

We find in the *Musnad* of al-Bazzar with an *isnad* which is questionable from the *hadith* related by Abu Hurayra ﷺ from the Prophet ﷺ who said, "The treasures of Allah are words. When Allah desires something, He says to it, ''Be' and it is." When Allah ﷻ desires something to happen, whether a gift or punishment or something else, He says to it, "'Be' and it is." How can it be conceived that this is a decrease? The same applies when He wants to create something. *"He says to it, 'Be,' and it is."* It is as He were saying, "*The likeness of 'Isa in Allah's sight is the same as Adam. He created him from earth and then He said to him, 'Be!' and he was.*" (3:59)

In one of the Israelite reports we find: "Allah Almighty revealed to Musa, peace and blessing be upon him, 'Musa, do not fear anything other than Me as long as I have power. My power is constant and is not cut off. Musa, do not be concerned about My provision ever as long as it is full and never runs out. Musa, do not be intimate with anyone other than Me as long as I am your intimate. When you seek Me, you will find Me. Musa, do not feel safe from My devising as long as you have not passed the *Sirat* to the Garden."

One of the wise said,

"Do not be humble to a creature in desire.
That will diminish your *deen*.
Seek provision from Allah with what is in His treasures.
Your provision lies between the *kaf* and the *nun*."[1]

He said, "O My slaves, it is your actions for which I call you to account and then repay you in full." He means that Allah ﷻ takes account of the actions of His slaves and then pays them in full by repaying them for them. *"Whoever does an atom's weight of good will see it, and whoever does an atom's weight of evil will see it."* (99:7-8) He also says, *"They will find there everything they did and your Lord will not wrong anyone at all.* " (18:49) The Almighty says, *"On the Day that each self finds the good it did and the evil it did present there in front of it, it will wish there were a great distance between it and them. Allah advises you to beware of Him. Allah is All-Gentle with His slaves."* (3:30) And also: *"On the Day that Allah raises up all of them together, He will inform them of everything they did. Allah has recorded it while they have forgotten it."* (58:6)

The *hadith* continues: "Then I will repay you in full." The apparent meaning is their full repayment on the Day of Rising as the Almighty says, *"You will be paid your wages in full on the Day of Rising."* (3:185) It is possible that it means that He will repay the slaves their actions in full in this world and the Next: as He says, *"Anyone who does evil will be repaid for it."* (4:123)

1. The Arabic word *"kun"* or "Be!" which is the word by which Allah creates.

It is related that the Prophet explained that as meaning that the believers are repaid for their evil deeds in this world while their good deeds are stored up for them in the Next World, where they will be paid their wages in full. As for unbelievers, the reward for their good actions is soon given to them in this world, but their evil actions are stored up for them and they will be punished for them in the Next World and will be given their repayment in full, good or evil. The evil is repaid in like measure without increase unless Allah pardons it. Good actions are multiplied by from ten to seven hundred times their like and to greater amounts whose number only Allah knows. As the Almighty says, *"The steadfast will be paid their wages in full without any reckoning."* (39:1)

The *hadith* goes on: "So anyone who finds good should praise Allah and anyone who finds something else should blame no one but himself." This indicates that all good is the favour of Allah to His slave without there being any question of his deserving it, and all evil comes from the son of Adam following his own passion. As the Almighty says, *"Any good thing that happens to you comes from Allah; any bad thing that happens to you comes from yourself."* (4:79) 'Ali said, "A slave should have no hope of anything except his Lord and should have no fear of anything except his wrong actions."

When Allah desires success and guidance for His slave, He helps him and gives him success in obeying Him. This is bounty and mercy from Him. When He wants to disappoint a slave, he entrusts him to his own devices and leaves him to it. So Shaytan deludes him by his heedlessness from remembering Allah and into following his passion. "His business is immoderation," and that is justice from Him. The proof is established against the slave by the revelation of the Book and the sending of the Messenger. There will not remain for anyone any argument against Allah after the Messengers have come.

The *hadith* says: "So anyone who finds good should praise Allah and anyone who finds something else should blame no one but himself." If what is meant is anyone who finds what is mentioned in this world, he is then commanded to praise Allah for what he finds by way of the repayment of righteous actions which is hastened in this world: as He says, *"What is with you comes to an end, but what is with Allah goes on for ever. Those who were steadfast will be recompensed according to the best of what they did."* (16:97) He is commanded to blame himself for any wrong actions he has done, whose consequences are tasted in this world, as the Almighty says, *"We will give them a taste of the nearer punishment before the greater punishment, so that perhaps they may turn back."* (32:21) When a believer is afflicted in this world by an affliction, he blames himself and calls on himself to return to Allah by repentance and asking forgiveness.

In the *Musnad* of Ahmad and the *Sunan* of Abu Dawud, it is reported that the Prophet ﷺ said, "When a believer is afflicted by illness and then Allah restores his health, it is expiation for his prior wrong actions and a warning for him for the rest of his life. When a hypocrite becomes ill and is restored to health, he is like a camel whose people have hobbled it and then released it. It does not know either why it was hobbled or why it was released." Salman al-Farisi said, "A Muslim is tried and that is a expiation for what he did in the past and an admonition for what remains of his life. An unbeliever is tested and he is like a camel which is released and does not know why it was released and hobbled."

If the *hadith* means that whoever finds good or other than it does so in the Next World, it is a statement that those who find good in the Next World praise Allah for that. Whoever finds other than that only blames himself when blame will not benefit him. So the words are in the form of a command which takes the form of a report. That is like the words of the Prophet ﷺ, "Whoever lies against me deliberately let him take his place in the Fire." This means that anyone who lies against him will take his place in the Fire.

Allah ﷻ reports that the people of the Garden praise Allah for the favours with which He has provided them: *"We will strip away all rancour in their breasts. Rivers will flow under them and they will say, 'Praise be to Allah who has guided us to this! We could not have been guided, had Allah not guided us.'"* (7:43) The Almighty says, *"They will say, 'Praise be to Allah who has fulfilled*

His promise to us and made us the inheritors of this land, letting us settle in the Garden wherever we will.'" (39:74) The Almighty also says, *"They will say, 'Praise be to Allah who has removed all sadness from us. Truly our Lord is Ever-Forgiving, Ever-Thankful: He who has lodged us, out of His favour, in the Abode of Permanence where no weariness or fatigue affects us.'"* (35:34-35)

Allah also tells us that the people of the Fire will blame themselves with the greatest vehemence. He says, *"When the matter is decided Shaytan will say, 'Allah made you a promise, a promise of truth, and I made you a promise and broke my promise. I had no authority over you. I merely I called you, and you responded to me. Therefore do not blame me but blame yourselves.'"* (14:22) The Almighty says, *"Those who rejected will be addressed resoundingly: 'Allah's hatred of you, when you were called to belief but then disbelieved, is even greater than your hatred of yourselves.'"* (40:10)

The righteous *Salaf* strove in righteous actions, in order to avoid criticism from their selves when actions fell short. In at-Tirmidhi it is reported as *marfu'* from Abu Hurayra: "There is no dead person who died without feeling regret. If he was a good-doer, he regrets not doing more, If he was an evildoer, he regrets that he did not reprove himself."

Masruq was told, "If only you would curtail some of the striving you do!" He said, "By Allah, if someone were to come to me tomorrow and inform me that Allah would not punish me, I would still strive in worship." He was asked, "Why is that?" He answered, "So that my self will not use me as an excuse if it enters the Fire, saying that I did not blame it! Have you not heard the words of Allah Almighty, *'No! I swear by the self-reproaching self?'* (75:1) People will criticise themselves until they go to the Hellfire of the *Zabaniya* (angels who guard Hell) and are cut off from what they desire; their hopes are cut off and mercy is removed from them, and each of them begins to blame himself."

'Amir ibn 'Abd Qays said, "By Allah, I will strive and then by Allah, I will strive. If I am saved, it is by the mercy of Allah. Otherwise I can only blame myself." Ziyad ibn 'Ayyash said to Ibn al-Munkadir and Safwan ibn Sulayman, "Gravity, gravity, and caution, caution. If the matter is not as we expect, it is excellent. Otherwise, you only have yourself to blame." Mutarrif ibn 'Abdullah used to say, "Strive in action. If things do not turn out as well as we hope regarding the mercy and forgiveness of Allah, it still has degrees. If the business is as terrible as we fear and are on guard against, we will not have to say, *'Our Lord! Take us out! We will act rightly, differently from the way we used to act!'* (35:37): we will say, 'We acted but it did not benefit us.'"[1]

1. Ibn Rajab, *Jami' al-'ulum wa'l-hikam*, p. 350.

Glossary

amir: commander, the source of authority in a situation

Amir al-Mu'minin: "the Commander of the Believers," the khalif or Caliph.

Ansar: the "Helpers", the people of Madina who welcomed and aided the Prophet ﷺ.

'Arafa: a plain fifteen miles to the east of Makka on which stands *Jabal ar-Rahma*, the Mount of Mercy. One of the essential rites of *hajj* is to stand on 'Arafa on the 9th of the month of Dhu'l-Hijja.

ayat: a verse of the Qur'an.

deen: the life-transaction, lit. the debt between two parties, in this usage between the Creator and creature.

faqih: pl. *fuqaha'*, a man learned in knowledge of *fiqh* who by virtue of his knowledge can give a legal judgement.

fatwa: an authoritative statement on a point of law.

fiqh: the science of the application of the *Shari'a*. A practitioner or expert in *fiqh* is called a *faqih*.

hadith: reported speech and/or action of the Prophet ﷺ.

hadith qudsi: those words of Allah on the tongue of His Messenger ﷺ which are not part of the Revelation of the Qur'an.

hasan: good, excellent; often used to describe a *hadith* which is reliable, but which is not as well authenticated as one which is *sahih* (sound).

hajj: the annual pilgrimage to Makka and its environs which is one of the five Pillars of Islam.

hanif: one who possesses the true religion innately.

haram: unlawful in the Shari'a.

Al-Harra: a stony tract of black volcanic rock east of Madina where a terrible battle took place in 63 AH (26 August 683) between the forces of Yazid I and 'Abdullah ibn az-Zubayr which ended in Madina being sacked and plundered.

Haruriyya: the first Kharijites or schismatics who separated themselves from 'Ali and based themselves at Harura', a town two miles from Kufa.

hima: a place of pasturage and water prohibited to the public. It was used for animals paid as *zakat* and for mounts used for *jihad.*

imam: Muslim religious or political leader; leader of Muslim congregational worship.

isnad: a tradition's chain of transmission from individual to narrator.

Jahannam: Hell.

Jahiliyya: the Time of Ignorance before the coming of Islam.

jihad: struggle, particularly fighting in the way of Allah to establish or defend Islam.

jinn: inhabitants of the heavens and the earth made of smokeless fire who are usually invisible.

Jumu'a: the assembly for the communal prayer on Friday.

Kharijites: the earliest sect, who separated themselves from the body of the Muslims and declared war on all those who disagreed with them, stating that a wrong action turns a Muslim into an unbeliever, and that they are more entitled to the caliphate.

khutba: a speech, and in particular a standing speech given by the Imam before the *Jumu'a* prayer and after the two *'Id* prayers.

marfu': 'elevated', a narration from the Prophet ﷺ mentioned by a Companion, e.g. "The Messenger of Allah ﷺ said..." without mentioning the name of the person who reported the words.

matn: the text of a *hadith.*

mawquf: 'stopped,' narration from a Companion. It can be elevated to *marfu'* if it is of the nature of "We were commanded to..." and the like.

mushrik: someone who commits *shirk.*

nafs: the self.

qadar: the decree of Allah, destiny

qunut: a supplication said in the prayer, particularly in the standing position after *ruku'.*

rak'at: a unit of the prayer consisting of a series of standings, bowing, prostrations and sittings.

ruh: the soul, vital spirit.

sadaqa: charitable giving in the Cause of Allah.

sahih: sound with no defects, used to describe an authentic *hadith.*

Salaf: the early generations of Muslims.

Shari'a: The legal modality of a people based on the revelation of their Prophet. The final *Shari'a* is that of Islam.

shaytan: a devil, particularly Iblis.

shirk: the unforgiveable wrong action of worshipping something or someone other than Allah or associating something or someone as a partner with Him.

Sirat: the narrow bridge which spans the Fire and must be crossed to enter Paradise.

Sunna: the customary practice of a person or group of people. It has come to refer almost exclusively to the normative practice of the Messenger of Allah ﷺ.

sura: chapter of the Qur'an.

Tabuk: a town in northern Arabia close to Jordan. In the ninth year after the Hijra, the Messenger of Allah ﷺ, hearing that the Byzantines were gathering a large army to march against the Muslims, led a large expedition, in his last campaign, on a long and arduous march across the desert to Tabuk, only to find the rumours premature.

takbir: saying "*Allahu Akbar*", "Allah is greater".

taqwa: awe or fear of Allah, which inspires a person to be on guard against wrong actions and eager to do actions which please Him.

tashriq: "drying meat in the sun", the 10th, 11th, 12th and 13th days of Dhu'l-Hijja when the pilgrims sacrifice their animals and stone the *jamras* (stone pillars) at Mina.

tawhid: the doctrine of Divine Unity.

witr: lit. "odd", a single *rak'at* prayed immediately after the *shaf'* which makes the number of *sunna* prayers uneven.

Zabaniya: "the violent thrusters", the angels who thrust people into Hellfire, who are nineteen in number.

zakat: a wealth tax, one of the five Pillars of Islam.

zindiq: a heretic whose teaching is a danger to the community or state.